Toronto Sketches 8

MIKE FILEY

Toronto Sketches

8

THE DUNDURN GROUP
TORONTO

Copy-Editor: Andrea Pruss
Design: Jennifer Scott
Printer: AGMV Marquis

National Library of Canada Cataloguing in Publication Data

Filey, Mike, 1941-
    Toronto sketches 8 : the way we were / Mike Filey.

ISBN 1-55002-527-9

1. Toronto (Ont.) — History. I. Title.

FC3097.4.F5495 2004   971.3'541   C2004-904464-8

1   2   3   4   5   08   07   06   05   04

We acknowledge the support of the **Canada Council for the Arts** and the **Ontario Arts Council** for our publishing program. We also acknowledge the financial support of the **Government of Canada** through the **Book Publishing Industry Development Program** and **The Association for the Export of Canadian Books,** and the **Government of Ontario** through the **Ontario Book Publishers Tax Credit** program, and the **Ontario Media Development Corporation's Ontario Book Initiative.**

Care has been taken to trace the ownership of copyright material used in this book. The author and the publisher welcome any information enabling them to rectify any references or credits in subsequent editions.

J. Kirk Howard, President

Printed and bound in Canada.
Printed on recycled paper.
www.dundurn.com

Dundurn Press
8 Market Street Suite 200
Toronto, Ontario, Canada
M5E 1M6

Gazelle Book Services Limited
White Cross Mills
Hightown, Lancaster, England
LA1 4X5

Dundurn Press
2250 Military Road
Tonawanda, NY
U.S.A. 14150

Table of Contents

Note: The date following each article is the day on which it first appeared in the *Sunday Sun*. Changes since the story's appearance have been added following the article, marked with an asterisk.

Fave Painting Tells a Story

I recently attended the unveiling of one of the Ontario Heritage Foundation's prestigious blue and gold commemorative plaques. The event, which took place in the historic Arcadian Court on the eighth floor of the Hudson Bay Company's downtown store, had a couple of purposes. One was to acknowledge the long history of the Robert Simpson Company (established in 1872 and purchased by The Bay in 1978) and the other, to honour the company's magnificent store that was erected at the southwest corner of Yonge and Queen streets in 1895.

The building, designed by local architect Edmund Burke, whose work can also be seen in the stately Prince Edward (Bloor Street) Viaduct, was the first in the city in which the internal steel girder skeleton rather than the external, usually brick or stone, walls bore the full weight of the structure. This factor not only allowed buildings of increased height, but did much to improve resistance to fire.

As I made my way from the elevator to the Arcadian Court I suddenly noticed a large painting on a nearby wall. It was a painting I had seen many, many years ago but couldn't remember just where. When I asked the Bay staff who might know the painting's background, I was introduced to Brenda Hobbs, the Hudson's Bay Company's Manager of Records and Historical Information.

Brenda told me that the painting, which had been purchased years earlier by the Simpson's company (and is part of collection of works pur-

Courtesy The Hudson's Bay Co.

Above: *The Lights of a City Street* by F.M. Bell-Smith. The 1894 view looks east along King Street at Yonge; the spire of St. James is in the distance.

Right: Same view, 2001.

chased by the company that will soon to be on display in the Bay store) used to hang in a less obvious location in the Simpson downtown store.

Suddenly it came to me. When I was a kid my mother would often take my brothers and me downtown to shop at the old Eaton's and Simpson's stores. We would take the streetcars that operated on the Bloor and Yonge routes. I was fascinated by streetcars (often sitting behind the motorman and pleading with him for the transfer stubs — wonder if kids still do that?).

During those many visits to the Simpson's store I must have seen this particular painting over and over. What made it stick in my mind must have been the two old streetcars in the view. I had rediscovered "my" painting. There we were, facing each other once again.

A little research on the internet and a pleasant conversation with Randy Speller at the Art Gallery of Ontario soon revealed that the work's creator was Frederick Marlett Bell-Smith. Born in London, England, in 1846, Bell-Smith immigrated to Canada at the age of twenty. He worked in a number of private art galleries in Montreal and Hamilton, and when photography became the rage, the young artist quickly earned a reputation as one of the country's best hand-tinting and retouching artists.

He later taught art in St. Thomas and London, Ontario, and for a time was principal of the Toronto Art School. Bell-Smith travelled extensively, drawing and painting for the Canadian Illustrated News and the Canadian Pacific Railway. He even had the opportunity of a private sitting with Queen Victoria, the first non-European to be given such an honour.

While Bell-Smith's works are far too numerous to list here, it is my humble opinion (though admittedly I am somewhat biased) that the one I rediscovered in The Bay store (and the one that appears with this column) is by far his best.

Titled *The Lights of a City Street*, this marvellous view of the busy Yonge and King street intersection was painted by Bell-Smith in 1894. Two of the new electric streetcars on the King route take on passengers at the corner while a bobby-helmeted policeman, draped in his rain cape, directs traffic (real traffic lights wouldn't appear in Toronto for another thirty-one years). To the right of the painting another officer patrols King Street. The building with the rounded front on the northeast corner was the Janes Building, which was replaced in 1914 by the present Royal Bank Building that now features a mattress store on its main floor. The building to the extreme right of the painting (southwest corner) was replaced in 1913 by the Dominion Bank Building (now TD Bank), which is now being converted to condominiums by entrepreneurs Harry Stinson and David Mirvish. And it's said that the portly gentleman being attacked by a flock of newspaper boys bears an amazing resemblance to the artist himself.

Bell-Smith died in 1923 as a result of a fall in the basement of his residence at 366 Jarvis Street.

January 21, 2001

Business Buried in the Past

If I were to ask which organization has been in business (and continues in business) here in Toronto longer than any other, what would
your answer be?

Some will answer the Hudson's Bay Company. After all, it was
established by royal charter way back in 1670, years before there was a
Toronto or even a country called Canada. As old as the company may
be, The Bay didn't enter the retail field until the 1880s and didn't actually appear here in our city until many years later, following its
takeover of the Morgan department store chain. Remember Morgan's
on Bloor Street West and in several of the suburban malls?

Consumers' Gas (now Enbridge — short for ENergy BRIDGE) is
another possible answer, although this company only goes back to
1848. It was established in response to local consumers' desire for a reli-
able and affordable source of coal gas.

And while it would be nice to consider Eaton's as an old-timer (the
original Eaton name goes back to 1869) the modern-day version of the
company, now spelled *eatons*, has only been around for a few months.
Across the street, Simpson's lost its identity when it was acquired by
the Hudson's Bay Company in 1978.

Some may answer Gooderham and Worts. Established in 1832, this
distilling company was on the Toronto waterfront so long many think it's
still in business. Unfortunately, G&W closed at the end of August 1990.

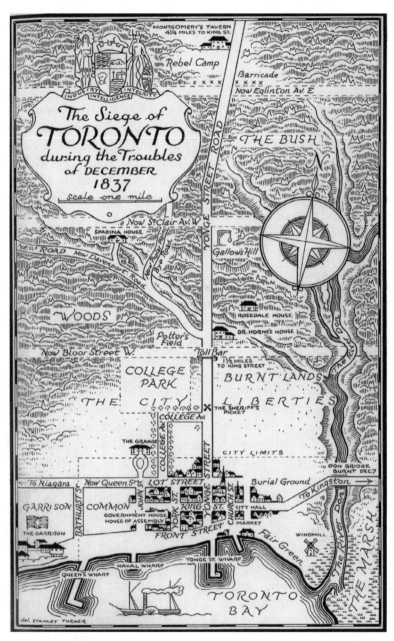

Map portraying Toronto and environs at the time of the Mackenzie Rebellion, December 1837. Note the location of Potter's Field, the community's first non-denominational cemetery, sitting on the outskirts of the city.

And that leaves one.

The honour of being the oldest enterprise still in operation in our city is an organization that was established exactly 175 years ago this coming Tuesday. Originally known as the York General Burying Grounds (remember, in 1826 Toronto was still eight years away from becoming a city, with the resulting change in name from York to Toronto), it is now known as the Mount Pleasant Group of Cemeteries. MPGC now administers a total of ten cemeteries, half of them in Toronto (Necropolis, Mount Pleasant, Prospect, York, and Pine Hills), the others in Vaughan (Beechwood), Richmond Hill (Elgin Mills), Brampton (Meadowvale), Oshawa (Thornton), and Pickering (Duffin Meadows). In addition, it manages five crematoria and oversees Canadian Memorial Services, better known as The Simple Alternative.

The origins of this historic organization go back to a time in our community when the two cemeteries then in existence were designated for only those citizens who adhered to either the Anglican or Roman Catholic faith. Only they were permitted a final resting place in their respective churchyards: that of the Anglicans around what is now St. James' Cathedral (a site now the subject of a redevelopment controversy) and that of the Roman Catholics in a graveyard adjacent to Old St. Paul's on Queen Street East.

For non-adherents, as well as the poor and strangers passing through the town, there was a major problem when the "final bell tolled." Where would the remains be buried?

To help alleviate this serious situation, one that became even more serious as the population of the prosperous community continued to grow, a group of public-spirited citizens met in late 1825 to arrange for the creation of the community's first public, non-denominational cemetery. Purchased for $300, what was known officially as the York General Burying Ground was established on a six-acre portion of the Elmsley farm, a site now defined as being at the northwest corner of the modern Yonge and Bloor intersection.

The first burial in this pioneer cemetery (that soon became known simply as Potter's Field from a biblical reference found in Matthew 27:7) took place on July 26, 1826. More than six thousand interments were carried in this cemetery out prior to its closure in early 1855.

In the years that followed, and in response to the area's ever-growing and diverse population, the successors to the York General Burying Grounds (Toronto General Burying Grounds, Toronto Trust Cemeteries, Commemorative Services of Ontario, and presently the Mount Pleasant

Group of Cemeteries — the latter name selected in recognition of the public's familiarity with the city's most beautiful cemetery) opened more properties while continuing to retain the traditions and integrity that have made it Toronto's oldest enterprise.

January 28, 2001

Marilyn Buoyed Our Hearts

Well, it's finally going to happen.

Nearly half a century after a young Toronto schoolgirl won the hearts of millions of Canadians from coast to coast, the remarkable story of Marilyn Bell's encounter with Lake Ontario will finally be told in a two-hour made-for-TV movie, *Heart: The Marilyn Bell Story*, on CBC stations this evening.

So excited were many Canadians with the young lady's achievement that if your name is Marilyn and you're in your late forties, there's a very good chance you were named in Miss Bell's honour.

Marilyn Bell was born in Toronto's St. Joseph's Hospital on October 19, 1937. As a teenager, she loved to swim and received much of her early training as a member of Alex Duff's Dolphinette Club, which practised at the now demolished Oakwood pool, not far from the busy St. Clair Avenue–Oakwood Avenue corner. Later, she joined the Lakeshore Swimming Club, where she caught the eye of the irascible Gus Ryder.

Marilyn was just sixteen years old and a student at Loretto College on Brunswick Avenue when she got it into her head that world-famous marathon swimmer Florence Chadwick wasn't the only person who could successfully complete the 23-mile (51.5-kilometre) crossing of Lake Ontario from the Wilson, N.Y., Coast Guard station to the CNE waterfront.

A small flotilla gathers around Marilyn Bell (her location in Lake Ontario is circled) as she struggles towards the CNE waterfront on the afternoon of September 9, 1954. The lack of any discernible landmarks on the city skyline made her destination point at the CNE waterfront difficult to locate. In fact, she came ashore just west of the Boulevard Club.

Swimming across Lake Ontario — which had never been done before — was the challenge that had been presented to Chadwick by Canadian National Exhibition officials as they sought to boost attendance at the 1954 celebration of the annual fair. If she succeeded, she'd receive a cash prize of $10,000; if she failed, the American swimming star wouldn't get a penny. Either way, the Ex couldn't lose. That $10,000 prize would be recovered easily from the fifty-cent entrance fee handed over by each of the thousands of extra visitors at the Ex who were eager to witness the American swimmer make history.

As the Exhibition dates approached, Chadwick's participation in the cross-lake swim was finally confirmed. Most believed that if she couldn't do it, no one could. After all, this was *the* Florence Chadwick, two-time conqueror of the English Channel.

Bell and her coach, Gus Ryder.

Young Marilyn had few credentials to suggest that she had any chance of completing the gruelling crossing. Sure, under the tutelage of her coach, Gus Ryder, the youngster had won a few races, the most impressive being the 1953 Atlantic City Marathon, where she became the first woman (and seventh overall) to finish the 26-mile (41.8-kilometre) event. But that swim was around an island and it was only twenty-six miles in length. For most of the lake swim she'd be out of sight of land, and it would be 6 miles (9.7kilometres) longer.

Spurred on by the CNE's decision to limit the cross-lake challenge to a single competitor, and an American at that, plus an arrogant statement that even if the young hometown swimmer was successful (a highly unlikely possibility) there would be no prize money from the Exhibition, Marilyn decided to give it her best try.

Everyone cheered as Chadwick entered the cold lake on the evening of September 8, 1954. Minutes later, Marilyn too was on her way, unnoticed except for her mother, father, coach, and a few friends in her pace boat. But soon the cold water proved to be too much for Chadwick, and she was taken, trembling, from the lake. Everyone believed that what had become known far and wide as the marathon swimming event of the century was over.

Then someone yelled, "Look over there!" Sure enough, someone else was still churning through the water — young Marilyn Bell! For more than twenty hours, Marilyn and the lake battled each other. For a time, Marilyn was in command, but as the hours passed, the lake appeared to be taking over. While the outcome of Marilyn's duel with Lake Ontario is now well known and a high point in Canadian history, the joyous conclusion was often very much in doubt at the time.

The whole story is nicely told in the CBC production *Heart: The Marilyn Bell Story*, which debuts this evening on Channel 6. Watch it and then tell me why the federal government hasn't awarded her the Order of Canada, or the province the Order of Ontario.

February 4, 2001

Coming to a Dead End

What's costing Toronto taxpayers nearly $40 million, yet will leave nothing to show for the huge expenditure? It's the demolition of that part of the Gardiner Expressway that continues east of the Don Valley Parkway, connecting with Leslie Street, 1.3 kilometres to the east. Once the dust has settled, this highway "orphan" will eventually be replaced by a new pair of on- and off-ramps that will connect with Lake Shore Boulevard.

Just where did this "orphan" come from? And did it ever have a purpose?

Historically, this portion of the Gardiner Expressway was to connect the expressway with a proposed new highway engineers were calling the Scarborough Expressway. A report issued in 1967 said this would be accomplished by extending the Gardiner Expressway (sections of which had opened across the city's waterfront between 1958 and 1963, with the connection with the new Don Valley Parkway opening in late 1964) easterly to Coxwell Avenue.

From here, the four-lane highway would curve north to the main CN line south of the Danforth and then follow this rail line east to Highland Creek where it would connect with Highway 401.

Seems simple enough, but with more than one thousand homes and businesses facing demolition to make way for the new limited-access highway, approval of the plans was less than a sure thing.

The Gardiner Expressway under construction at the mouth of the Don River in 1963. Oil storage tanks, rail yards, and industries occupied lands on which a community to be known as Ataratiri was to be developed. It wasn't. The link that would have connected the Gardiner with the proposed Scarborough Expressway can be seen at the lower right.

Over the years, these plans were altered to limit the need for demolitions. But with the provincial government's June 1971 decision to cancel the Spadina Expressway, the fate of the Scarborough superhighway was pretty well sealed.

Revival attempts were made over the ensuing years, but, in the words of Councillor Brian Ashton, the proposed Scarborough Expressway now lies dead in the "expressway cemetery."

February 11, 2001

* The route through Scarborough that would have connected the Gardiner with Highway 401 in the northeast part of the city was never built. The section of the connecting link seen in the view was recently demolished.

Auto Shows a Toronto Tradition

For many, the highlight of winter in Toronto is the annual Canadian International AutoShow (CIAS). This year's show runs daily until next Saturday, with a huge assortment of vehicles — old, new, and several of the concept variety — filling the massive exhibit space in SkyDome and the Metro Convention Centre.

The popularity of the CIAS should come as no surprise. Torontonians were familiar with automobile shows as early as 1906, when a selection of autos (described by many as "horseless carriages") was exhibited at the now demolished University Avenue Armouries.

Over the years other shows were held, with one of the most interesting being a display presented in Simpson's Arcadian Court in 1929. Getting the vehicles in and out was accomplished by hoisting them to the roof of the old building on Richmond Street, and then, after constructing a ramp, pushing them into the new Simpson's store addition.

For many years, the most popular attraction at the annual CNE was a car show that initially occupied the old Transportation Building at the west end of the grounds. (This building, in the guise of the Spanish Building, burned to the ground in 1974.) In 1929, the show moved to the new Automotive Building, just inside the Princes' Gates, where it was an annual feature until the late 1960s.

The eventual demise of the CNE car show was predictable. While still popular with the Ex-going public, it was less so for the car dealers who

The twentieth century was only a few years old when a clutch of pioneer automobile owners showed up at City Hall to voice their concerns about such serious matters as speed limits and potholes.

manned the booths. With car manufacturers constantly moving their new-car unveiling dates later into the year, it wasn't long before those debuts occurred after the CNE had closed. This resulted in the Ex featuring a building full of year-old cars that nobody was interested in buying.

With the end of the CNE car show, the city was left without a similar event for several years until the Toronto Automobile Dealers Association sponsored a new event called Auto Show '74. Nearly 80,000 people paid the $2.50 admission to visit the inaugural edition of what would eventually become today's CIAS.

That first show, which incidentally was also in February, occupied one hundred square feet of floor space at the Toronto International Centre near the International Airport. It was basically a "new car only" show that featured a sprinkling of antique autos from the Craven Collection. There were no car-related displays.

This year, show officials are anticipating 260,000 visitors who will pay $15 to view 800,000 square feet of exhibits presented by 140 exhibitors. The huge show is billed as a "total automotive experience."

February 18, 2001

Looking For an Even Better Way

As municipal and provincial politicians and their respective bureaucrats argue over who is responsible for the massive debt incurred by the city over recent years, one area up for review is the proliferation of public transit authorities throughout the Greater Toronto Area. Some would say that by combining these seventeen autonomous authorities into one entity, the taxpayers would save a bundle of money.

One of the arguments in favour of combining the various transit operators is the undeniable fact that the GTA is, in fact, one sprawling community. Each day, hundreds of thousands of its citizens journey from one jurisdiction to another and back. Some even travel from one jurisdiction through another to another and back. Is it time for a single operating authority for the GTA?

While I don't have the definitive answer, I can point to occasions in our city's history when the same kind of situation existed, albeit not nearly as complex and widespread as the problem we're faced with today. Nevertheless, perhaps we can learn from the past (now there's a novel idea!).

Today's Toronto Transit Commission began operations exactly eighty years ago this year. Known in the beginning as the Toronto Transportation Commission (Transit replaced Transportation with the opening of the Yonge subway on March 30, 1954), it had been created

Courtesy TTC Archives

In the summer of 1924, the TTC was given the authority to operate streetcar service on four York Township thoroughfares (Oakwood and Eglinton avenues and Rogers and Weston roads). This photo shows the opening of the Oakwood route (running from Oakwood and St. Clair to Eglinton and Gilbert) on November 19, 1924, an early example of the consolidation of transit operations under one authority.

to improve the public transportation nightmare that bedevilled the citizens of the day.

Private operators were more interested in the bottom line than in providing a safe and convenient service. To be frank, while safety was under the watchful eye of the government, convenience as far as the passengers were concerned usually wasn't even discussed.

Then, with the arrival of the TTC's first modern, red streetcars on September 1, 1921, the wheels were set in motion to unify nine separate systems that had been providing inconvenient, expensive, and less-than-satisfactory transportation service in, and around, the fast-growing city for years.

Within a short time, riders in such outlying districts as Oakwood, Lambton, and Weston in York Township and Birch Cliff, Birchmount, and West Hill in Scarborough Township, as well as those in the far-

A new GO Train poses for its portrait just a few months before regular service begins on the Lakeshore line. Note the rather unobstructed skyline that features (left to right) the Royal York Hotel, the first TD Bank tower, and the Bank of Commerce (now Commerce Court North) in April 1967.

thest reaches of the city (the Junction, Davisville, Eglinton, and Bedford Park) were afforded the ability to ride from place to place on vehicles operated by a single authority: the TTC.

To be sure, the new TTC had its failings, but it was well on its way to becoming one of the world's great public transit operators. Then, on January 1, 1954, the TTC underwent another change. With the establishment of the new Municipalities of Metropolitan Toronto, a federation of the city and twelve surrounding municipalities, the Commission's mandate was broadened considerably.

Prior to the formation of Metro, the TTC had provided transit service for a city that covered a mere thirty-five square miles. Now it would be responsible for all public transit within the 240 square miles known as Metro Toronto. As part of this consolidation of services, such well-known bus operators as Hollinger, Danforth, Roseland, West York, and others vanished, their routes becoming the responsibility of the "new" TTC.

I wonder if the creation of a GTA-wide public transit authority wouldn't simply be the next logical step in the evolution of the area's transportation needs. On the other hand, perhaps this approach is just too simplistic. After all, where would all the officials go?

February 25, 2001

Dial-Up Phone Changes

For the past two months some nice lady in a small office in a Bell building somewhere has been warning us that phone calls will soon require dialling a total of ten digits ... or else. Well, zero hour has arrived. Starting tomorrow, the area code 416 will be mandatory when dialling all local calls. If you don't use it, that nice lady ain't goin' to help you no more.

Seems that with the almost 6 million phones and their extensions, analog and digital cell phones, faxes, etc. presently in use throughout the 416 area, the simple fact is that Bell is running out of telephone numbers. The addition of a new prefix, 647, allows the introduction of a whole bunch of new ones. And there's even a problem up in 905 country. To help alleviate that situation a new 289 prefix will be added on June 9. As troublesome as trying to remember to add that d#@7! three-number prefix might be, it's probably less confusing than some of the changes Bell made in years gone by.

For instance, hundreds of Toronto customers were baffled in 1881 when the prefix MAIN was added to a phone number that up until then had been just four numbers. Over the following years other prefixes were added so that eventually everyone had to add the first two letters of a prefix to the four numbers. Phew!

Some of the earliest prefixes were NOrth (introduced in 1884), JUnction (1892), PArkdale (1890), BEach (1903), and ADelaide (1911). As the years passed others such as WAverley, REdfern, HArgrave,

Courtesy City of Toronto Archives

In the summer of 1924, police officers at No.10 station, Main Street and Swanick Avenue, learn the intricacies of the new dial telephone.

HOward, BElmont, LLoydbrook, and ROdney were added. Those prefixes also identified in what part of the city the subscriber resided. It became a game to guess where people lived by their telephone number. My family lived near Bloor and Bathurst and we had a somewhat middle-class MElrose 2154. When we moved to north Toronto our new number was a more high-class HYland 7463.

Increasing demand for telephones in the early 1950s forced the company to change local telephone numbers from the six-digit type (first two letters of the prefix plus four numbers) to seven digits (two letters of the prefix and five numbers). The first seven-digit numbers used were EMpire 3 and EMpire 4. Our HYland number went to HUdson 9 in 1953.

It was with a real sense of loss for many when the names that made up prefixes were replaced with a mundane set of numbers. Many have never known the pleasure of being identified as RUssell 1, 2, 3, 7, or 9. One of the biggest changes in the way calls were placed occurred in 1924. This one had nothing to do with telephone numbers, but rather with the instrument itself. It was on the evening of July 19 of that year that the dial telephone was introduced to Bell subscribers in Toronto. Up until that time, customers simply picked up the phone and asked the operator to connect them with a certain number. With costs and customers increasing at a rapid pace, the company decided to convert the city system to automatic using the GROVER exchange in the city's east end as a testing ground. All subscribers in that exchange would henceforth do the connecting themselves using the new dial telephone.

To get them ready for the change-over Bell sent written "how-to" instructions to its GROVER customers. In addition, a series of "open houses" at the telephone office on Main Street were held during which subscribers could drop by for a "hands on" course in using the new instrument. In addition, special instruction classes were held to help the firefighters and police officers assigned to the nearby fire hall and police station learn how to use the new dial phones.

March 4, 2001

No Getting Away from Them

As sure as Toronto winters bring salty pant cuffs and overcoat zippers that refuse to zip, so too does winter bring those darn potholes. In fact, ever since 1889, the year city workers began putting down asphalt to smooth out such thoroughfares as Bay (Front to King), Jarvis (Queen to Bloor), St. George (Bloor to Bernard), and Wellington (Yonge to Church), potholes have been a feature of our city's winter streetscape.

Over the years, aging pavements, ever-increasing traffic volumes, and heavier and heavier vehicles combined with frequent late winter freeze/thaw weather cycles have all contributed to making potholes an inevitable as the arrival of the daffodils and hyacinths.

A quick perusal of old city newspapers on microfilm in the Sun News Research Centre's archives revealed that while every winter has had its fair share of potholes, the year 1962 was bad enough to prompt the old *Toronto Telegram* newspaper to institute the "Pothole Patrol." Readers would call the paper daily with a description of the worst pothole they had seen or had been immersed in that day. Whether the hole was filled or not was not reported. However, the reader submitting the best of the worst got his or her name in the paper, and that probably didn't hurt newspaper sales.

A few years ago, a rather interesting way to help offset the cost of repairing potholes was devised by the city council of Falls River, Oregon. The holes were graded as either of the small or large variety.

Now that's a pothole!! This undated photo of some unidentified Toronto street is from the City of Toronto Archives.

Citizens were then offered the chance of sponsoring the repair, ten dollars for the small, twenty dollars for the large. And what was in it for the sponsor? Well, once the hole was patched, the crew spray-painted on the patch these few words: "This pothole repaired through the courtesy of" followed by the sponsor's name.

Back here in Toronto, the city's Transportation Department ask that you report major potholes to them so that repairs can be effected. Please call 416-599-9090, #164 and give them the precise location.

By the way, while I was going through the old newspapers I came across the following pair of news items, each somewhat reminiscent of what's going on today.

Just as some politicians are trying to ease the budget crunch by closing the High Park Zoo and Riverdale Farm and sending the animals to the Toronto Zoo in north Scarborough, back in 1942 a similar cost-saving measure was proposed by city politician of the day Lewis Duncan. His idea, however, was a bit more radical in that the controller suggested closing the city zoo in Riverdale Park entirely. He suggested that the city's humane society could "dispose" of the zoo's two old lions and one old tiger and then take the bears and wolves "and any others that could take care of themselves" to Kapuskasing where they'd be set free. Fortunately, Duncan's proposal didn't get a seconder.

In another story from the same year, the TTC was adamant that the city begin investigating plans to build a pair of subways (the Yonge and Queen lines) as well as create four major traffic arteries to free the city from future traffic gridlock.

March 11, 2001

Downtown Living at Its Best

Have you noticed the amount of space in the Toronto papers being devoted to the subject of real estate? Each week, there are dozens and dozens of pages featuring stories and ads on new houses, resales, or those ubiquitous condominium towers. To highlight just how busy the market is, a recent edition of a Saturday paper listed nearly 150 housing projects throughout the city that are either under construction or in the planning stages. Interestingly, of this remarkable number, approximately one-third are located in the downtown area.

It really wasn't all that long ago that downtown Toronto was simply the place where people went to work, to shop, to see a first-run movie, or, once in a while, to dine at a fine restaurant. But to actually live downtown, well, that was regarded as a social stigma.

It wasn't always that way. In fact, living in the heart of the city was the norm back in the 1800s. For a time, thoroughfares such as Wellington Street (west of Simcoe), little Widmer Street, and, in particular, Mercer Street were lined with some of Toronto's classiest residences. Not far away, at the northeast corner of King and Bay streets, quite literally the heart of the city of the day, was a structure regarded by many (including John George Howard of High Park fame and pioneer city architect) as the "finest and most elegant town house in the entire city."

The house was erected between 1851 and 1853 as the residence of William Cawthra, a prominent local businessman and wealthy financier

The Cawthra House (disguised here as the Sterling Bank) gave a sense of residential dignity to the King and Bay intersection for nearly a century. Photo *circa* 1925.

who had served his community as both alderman and school trustee. William was born in 1801, the son of Joseph Cawthra, who immigrated to Upper Canada from Yorkshire two years later. Upon his arrival, Joseph was granted a large parcel of land in the hinterland well west of the Town of York near the mouth of the Credit River, a location we now know as Port Credit. A nar-

Postcard issued soon after the opening of the new Bank of Nova Scotia head office in 1951. This modern skyscraper was erected on the site of the old Cawthra House.

row dirt road was eventually cut through part of his property. That thoroughfare was subsequently known (and still is today) as Cawthra Road. The Cawthra family soon moved to the Town of York (Toronto) where son William received his education at the Home District Grammar School. He then went to work in his father's apothecary and general store at the northwest corner of King and Sherbourne streets in the business section of the young community.

William married Sarah Crowther in 1849 and the couple moved into a small cottage near the corner of today's Bloor and Jarvis streets in the rural Village of Yorkville. As William's business and real estate fortunes continued to swell he decided to construct a proper city home close to his business contacts, choosing a building site on property he owned at the King and Bay intersection. It's believed the architect was William Irving, a junior in the office of Joseph Sheard. The house was built of substantial blocks of light-coloured sandstone with beautifully cut stone mouldings all in the Greek Revival style. Its main entrance was originally on Bay Street, though in later years that was changed to a King Street location. Cawthra lived and carried out his business dealings in the house until his death in 1880. His widow remained in the house for another five years until moving to her new residence in the posh upper Jarvis Street neighbourhood.

By then, the King-Bay intersection had become completely commercialized in nature and the house changed roles, first as the site of the Toronto Branch of the Molson Bank and later the Head Office of the Sterling Bank. Later, the house was acquired by its next door neighbour, the Canada Life Assurance Co. In 1929, Canada Life announced that it would build a beautiful new building on University Avenue north of Queen. The historic Cawthra House was then put on the market and eventually purchased by the Bank of Nova Scotia, who too were about to build a new head office. There was no question, the old house would have to go.

But not quite yet. The Depression hit and the bank's plans were put on hold. A number of ideas to save the old house began to surface, one of which would have seen the impressive King and Bay street facades taken down and reassembled on the grounds of the Royal Ontario Museum. But pride in the city's past just wasn't strong enough, and in 1946 the historic mansion was demolished. Within a few years, the new Bank of Nova Scotia stood on the site.

March 18, 2001

WWII Hit Close to Home

Several weeks ago I was the guest speaker at a dinner meeting of a local branch of the Royal Canadian Legion. During the meal, I sat with several veterans of the Second World War. Two had served overseas while two others were active on the homefront. As happens when old comrades get together the stories flew fast and furious. Many, of course, had to do with events that took place throughout the European theatres of war. I was especially intrigued, however, by the comments describing how the war, in its early stages, was affecting Torontonians — who, though thousands of miles from the action, were aware that things were not going well. In fact, German air raids on their beloved city were a distinct possibility. That evening's conversation prompted me to become a citizen of Toronto in the year 1942, perhaps the scariest of all in the five-year conflict.

I began reading back issues of the old *Telegram* newspaper captured on microfilm in the Sun News Research Centre. To say the least, some of the war stories made me feel that had the events of that year continued, by the time I reached high school (I was only a year old in 1942) I would be reading and speaking German on a day-to-day basis, with English relegated to simply one of the subjects under the heading "foreign languages." To give some idea of the seriousness of the situation that year, in July 1942 Ontario Premier Mitchell Hepburn predicted that it wouldn't be long before the Japanese, who were winning

Torontonians stand mesmerized as army vehicles on manoeuvres charge through the Bay and Queen intersection in the summer of 1941.

battle after battle throughout the Pacific, would be able to bomb cities on the west coast of Canada and the States at will. Once that happened, how long would it be before cities in the interior, cities like Toronto and Hamilton, came under attack?

In an effort to at least show they were ready if and when those air raids came, officials of the Simpson's store at Yonge and Queen boasted in a full-page newspaper ad that they had held a mock air raid test and found that they were able to evacuate the store in less than eight minutes. Toronto underwent simulated air raid attacks as well, complete with city-wide blackouts. Even the bulbs illuminating the clock in the City Hall tower were ordered extinguished for the duration. The blackout test on May 8, 1942, was especially disconcerting for Torontonians who had heard earlier that day that a German prisoner of war had escaped from the camp in Bowmanville. News announcers suggested that he was probably prowling the darkened city streets. However, the bad guy was soon found and returned to the camp. The problems associated with mandatory rationing were also becoming facts of life. With quantities of sugar, tea, and coffee in short supply the government decreed that their availability would be strictly controlled through the use of coupons that would soon be issued to all citizens. By August, vacationing teachers were busy in various rooms in Jarvis Collegiate Institute assembling the first 1,277,000 of the new coupon books. And it wasn't just individuals who faced restrictions. Restaurants were ordered to serve customers only one cup of coffee or tea with meals. Under no circumstances would refills be permitted. In 1942, submarine warfare had seriously depleted gasoline reserves. So much so that effective October 1, 1942, owners of vehicles that were used only for personal transportation would be limited to between sixty-four and seventy-two gallons (depending on the size of the car) during the following six-month period.

Eaton's and Simpson's, along with a few city bakeries and dairies, found an interesting way to help alleviate this rationing problem. Their deliveries would be made by truck as well as by horse-drawn delivery wagon. But that prompted another problem: the sound of clip-clopping horseshoes on city pavements. Rubber covers over the shoes had been introduced before the war to alleviate the problem, but now rubber was impossible to find. So the noise became another war time aggravation. Another indication that things were in a serious state came late in the summer of 1942 when CNE officials announced that the tradition of going to the Ex, something that had occurred without interruption since 1879, would end. Effective immediately, the CNE grounds would become a military camp to accommodate the country's growing military forces. Within days, the air force had taken over the Coliseum with army personnel entrenched in the Horse Palace and the navy all ship-shape in the Automotive Building.

Throughout the fall of 1942, convoys of Jeeps, military trucks, and even tanks were to be seen on city streets as they made their way to realistic sham battles in city parks such as Riverdale and Eglinton. There was even an attack on "enemy" troops dug in at Sunnyside. The attacking Canadian force stormed the beach from boats moored in Humber Bay and quickly defeated "Jerry." While these raids may have brought the war closer to home, many city families already knew the war was real. The August 19 raid on Dieppe, France, had resulted in 3,367 Canadian casualties; one-sixth of that number were from Toronto homes.

March 25, 2001

WWII Heroes Boost Morale

In last week's column I wrote about just how serious the war situation was for the Allies during its early stages and the impact the numerous enemy victories in both the European and Far East theatres of war were having on morale here at home.

Local news reports suggested that unless there was an all-out effort by Canadians it wouldn't be long before Japanese bombers were attacking cities and towns along the country's west coast. Soon, Halifax, Montreal, and Toronto too would be under attack by German war planes. Practice air raids and city-wide blackouts became serious interruptions to everyday activities.

To be sure, there were a few bright spots. Frequently, those same doom and gloom news sources would run stories intended to provide some morale boosting. One individual who got a lot of attention was Douglas Bader, a Royal Air Force pilot who, in a pre-war training mission, had crashed. His injuries resulted in the amputation of both legs. Nevertheless, Bader's dogged determination, plus a pair of artificial legs, soon saw the young Brit back in the cockpit. Eventually, the Allied newspapers were to trumpet that it was this kind of determination, a determination typical of the harassed British people, that would eventually see the country victorious over its enemies.

In the fall of 1939 Great Britain went to war with Germany. Less than a year later, the country suffered its first major defeat, the debacle at

Dunkirk. With the country reeling, Douglas Bader was assigned command of 242 Squadron, a unit that was primarily made up of Canadian flyers. He quickly converted what up until then had been a somewhat rag-tag, leaderless group of young men into what would become one of the war's most successful and decorated squadrons.

Another year passed in a war that was full of bad news for the British. When it looked like things couldn't get worse it was reported that Douglas Bader, now Wing Commander Bader of Tangmere Squadron, was missing in action. While this was bad news, it wasn't as bad as first thought. Bader had been forced to parachute from his Spitfire after it collided with an enemy ME-

Photo courtesy Toronto Sun Archives

John Nickleson, RCAF pilot and North Toronto Collegiate grad, stands in front of his Blenheim fighter-bomber, somewhere in England, 1941.

109. He descended to earth minus his legs, which had been firmly wedged in the Spitfire's badly smashed foot controls. Once on the ground, he was quickly captured and transported to a local German hospital where the doctor was stunned when he examined Bader. "You have no legs," blurted the doctor. "They came off when I left my plane," countered the wing commander, tongue firmly implanted in his cheek.

Bader requested that his captors scour the wreckage of his plane for possible recovery and reuse of the artificial limbs. When only one was found, he had the audacity to ask that another be sent from England. The Germans, apparently in awe of this smug yet resolute RAF pilot, agreed.

Here's where the story gets interesting for the people here in Toronto, who were eagerly scanning the papers for some good news.

While every member of Bader's squadron pleaded to carry out the mission, the local papers proudly announced that Sergeant-Pilot J.H. Nickleson from Toronto had been given the assignment.

In civilian life John Nickleson lived with his parents at 148 Roselawn Avenue, a modest house a short walk from the busy Yonge and Eglinton corner. In the early summer of 1940, just two weeks after his graduation from North Toronto Collegiate Institute, the eighteen-year-old decided to join the RCAF. Less than six months later he went overseas and in the summer of 1941 flew his Blenheim bomber in one of the RAF's first daylight air raids on Germany. Returning to base, he was given the Bader assignment, which he carried out to perfection.

One month later Sergeant-Pilot Nickleson was killed in action. He was only nineteen. Young John's name is proudly listed on his high school's Role of Honour.

April 1, 2001

Leafs Scored First Cup in '32

Hey, you know what happened for the first time sixty-nine years ago tomorrow? Here's a hint. It's something that's happened a total of eleven times since then, though anyone under the age of thirty-four will have never experienced the excitement it brings.

Give up?

Well, it was on April 9, 1932, that the Toronto Maple Leaf hockey team won its very first Stanley Cup. Now, that's not to say it was the first time a team from Toronto had won Governor General Lord Stanley's coveted trophy. No, that had happened twice before. In both 1918 and 1922 teams from our city won the cup. The first time it was a team known as the Toronto Arenas (the fellows played in Mutual Street Arena) who were victorious, the second time it was the St. Pats. On both occasions, the vanquished team was the Vancouver Millionaires.

On February 14, 1927, the Toronto team was renamed the Toronto Maple Leafs and for the next few years played rather so-so hockey. In the 1931–32 season, however, things got better with the team finishing third in the two-division (Canadian and American), eight-team league. In the quarter-finals "total goals, two-game" series our guys scored six, compared to only two scored by the guys from Chicago. In the semi-final, again a "total goals, two-game" series, the Leafs beat the Maroons from Montreal four goals to three.

Joe Primeau played centre and had the most points (fifty in forty-six games) on the Leafs first Stanley Cup–winning team. In a newspaper ad that appeared the day after the team won the cup, he announced he liked Buckingham cigarettes.

Then it was on to the finals. The Rangers had defeated the Canadiens in their series and now faced the Leaf team in a "best of five games" series. Again the Leafs were victorious, this time in convincing fashion, winning three straight.

The final game in the series, and the one that clinched the Stanley Cup for the Toronto Maple Leaf for the first time, was played exactly sixty-nine years ago tomorrow.

A popular annual attraction in Toronto, and one that's been around since 1951, is the National Home Show. A mainstay at many of the early shows was a fellow who became known nation-wide as Mr. Fixit, the late Peter Whittall.

Born in Toronto in 1907, Peter accompanied his family when they moved to rural Manitoba. It was here that the youngster went to school and eventually got his first job with the CBC as a writer of a daily soap opera produced by the Corporation's Farm Department.

In 1950, CBC transferred Peter to Toronto, where he continued to work on farm items for radio. It wasn't long, however before his hobby fixing things around the house came to the attention of the producers of *Living*, one of the pioneer talk shows on the CBC's newly-established Toronto television station CBLT, Channel 9 (the station's move down the dial to Channel 5 didn't happen until 1956).

Canadian TV's original Mr. Fix-It, Peter Whittall, with Miss Formica at the Home Show sometime in the 1960s. For what it's worth, the Formica Company was started in 1913 and originally made electrical insulators out of ... wait for it ... mica.

On *Living*, which was hosted by vivacious Elaine Grand, Peter described in his unique down-home, easy-to-understand fashion some interesting (or not) do-it-yourself project. The popularity of his visits soon resulted in CBC awarding Peter his own fifteen-minute do-it-yourself show. "Mr. Fixit" was seen on Saturday evenings until 1964. Peter passed away in the fall of 1974.

April 8, 2001

Toronto Shows Off Its Easter Finery

One of the oldest traditions in our city is the annual Easter Day Parade. Though now held in a part of the city known as the Beach (an historic appellation that referred to the one long beach that ran along the water's edge in the "cottage country" east of the city), the parade actually got its start along the city's western waterfront. How Sunnyside actually got its name remains a bit of a mystery. The easy answer is that John George Howard, of High Park fame, built a summer villa on the sunny side of a hill somewhere in the vicinity of the modern St. Joseph's Hospital on The Queensway. Calling the place "Sunnyside" could have been spontaneous. However, there's another possibility for the term, and one that is much more romantic.

When Howard eventually sold his villa, the purchaser was an American-born industrialist who had come to Toronto to sell his stoves. The newcomer was a huge fan of Washington Irving, the author of numerous books, including *The Legend Of Sleepy Hollow* and *Rip Van Winkle*. In fact, he was such a fan that some say he named his new home Sunnyside in honour of Irving's residence, which still overlooks the Hudson River near the pretty little community of Tarrytown in New York State. It was then that the house became known as Sunnyside, and not long after the same name was used to identify the surrounding area. In the late nineteenth century city folk, looking for a place to escape the heat and smoke, found the Sunnyside shoreline. Before long crowds

An early edition of the Easter Parade along the water's edge at Sunnyside, *circa* 1900.

A quartet of young Toronto lasses parade in their stylish shortie coats in the 1950 Easter Parade along the Sunnyside Amusement Park boardwalk. Recognize anyone?

thronged the wooden boardwalk, many dressed in their smartest togs. With the opening of Sunnyside amusement park in 1922 officials saw the institution of a formal Easter Parade — a great way to attract crowds to the amusements and the hot dog and Honey Dew stands. When the park's future looked in doubt and attendance slipped, the parade was relocated to Bloor Street near Bay. In recent years, Toronto's Easter Parade has been a feature of the Beaches, oops, the Beach.

April 15, 2001

Toronto's Diamond Dreams

*B*aseball's Back In Town! is the title of Lou Cauz's fascinating book detailing the history of baseball here in our city. It also happens to be a statement of fact. Our Blue Jays are off and running once again, and who knows, perhaps the boys will experience the good fortunes of those special two years, 1992 and 1993.

Lou's book was published just as the deal to get Toronto into the major leagues was being completed, and though it's long out-of-print I'm sure copies can be viewed in research libraries throughout the city. By the way, remember the name of the first player to be signed by the Jays? Baltimore shortstop Bob Bailor.

Contrary to what some may think, watching a baseball game had been a popular pastime around this city long before when the newborn Blue Jays team came up to bat for the very first time that cold Thursday afternoon, April 7, 1977.

Historically, the first mention of the game of baseball being played here in Toronto appears in an 1859 edition of the *Globe* newspaper. It was a brief article and simply stated, "A number of young men in this city have organized themselves into a baseball club called the Canadian Pioneers. They practice every Monday afternoon at 4:00 p.m. at the University Grounds."

It's a pretty safe assumption that the Pioneers drew a crowd of spectators who were as intrigued by the process of playing this "game"

Maple Leaf Stadium, at the foot of Bathurst Street, was home field for Toronto's International League team from 1926 to 1967.

called baseball as they were by the talent involved in the batting, throwing, and catching of a small ball. Nevertheless, it was on that afternoon 142 years ago that a new pastime, a pastime that would eventually be shared by thousands of Torontonians, was born.

Initially, the game was only played by a small clutch of dedicated amateurs who couldn't care less what most Torontonians thought of the game. Being an imported "sport" from south of the border it was regarded by many in less than glowing terms. In fact, one local writer suggested that while cricket was for the elders and lacrosse for young socialites, baseball was simply a game for the community's undesirable.

It took some time before the game had gained enough fans to give it some legitimacy. Then, in 1876, a local team known as the Clippers was invited to join the Canadian Professional Baseball League. Torontonians had finally been smitten by the pro baseball bug. But not smitten badly enough it seems. The league folded after one year, and another seven would pass before another team from Toronto had the nerve to enter a professional league.

In 1885, the Canadian League was established. It consisted of teams from Toronto, Guelph, London, and two from Hamilton with

1886 DIAMOND JUBILEE 1949

ENTRANCE

Just as a stylized Blue Jay is the logo of our present team, Handlebar Hank became the symbol of the old Maple Leafs team. It was designed by Guy Leslie, an electrical repairman who received $100 for his idea.

the local boys playing on the Lacrosse Grounds at the northwest corner of Jarvis and Wellesley streets. Although the inaugural season was a success (gate receipts amounted to $8,500, while players' salaries came to $4,231) the teams from Toronto and Hamilton decided to join another league, one with several teams representing American cities.

It was known as the International League, and it was in this association that the Toronto Maple Leaf team played (except for the period between 1891 and 1895) for almost eight decades.

During the team's existence, a variety of ball parks were considered home field. First was little Sunlight Park (southwest of the Queen and Broadview corner), followed by Hanlan's Point on Toronto Island. A fire then forced a temporary sojourn to another small field, this one on Fraser Avenue north of the CNE Grounds, prior to a return to a larger stadium at the Island. In 1926, the team moved to the newly constructed $750,000 Maple Leaf Stadium located on Fleet Street (now Lake Shore Boulevard West) at the foot of Bathurst Street (This accounts for the name Stadium Road on a nearby thoroughfare.) The team played here until fan indifference forced the organization into bankruptcy in 1967.

A decade passed, and along came the newly franchised Toronto Blue Jays of the American League. By the way, initial reaction to the team's name was less than positive. Some suggested it was too effeminate. If the name selection had gone differently, we might be cheering for the Toronto Battlers, Blue Bats, or Mounties.

April 22, 2001

Looking After Our Veterans

Several weeks ago, my wife and I had the pleasure of attending the official opening of a new care facility on the rambling campus of the Sunnybrook & Women's College Health Sciences Centre (Women's College and the Orthopaedic and Arthritic Institute amalgamated with Sunnybrook in the summer of 1998) on Bayview Avenue. To be known as the Dorothy Macham Home, this state-of-the-art project, the first of its kind in Canada, will serve as home for ten armed forces veterans who suffer from aggressive behavioral difficulties due to dementia.

While Sunnybrook & Women's College is now known primarily for a variety of public health care programs, the hospital actually opened its doors in 1948 as a medical facility devoted to the needs of Canada's returning war wounded. Though difficult to understand today, the birth of Sunnybrook Hospital was not without difficulty. Back then the federal government was less than receptive to the idea of building a brand new veterans' hospital. Officials believed that a simple makeover of the old facility on Christie Street would suffice. The public was not impressed. After all, they argued, Christie Street was itself a makeover of what had been a cash register factory. It was surrounded by noisy factories and even noisier steam trains that rattled back and forth over the busy CPR main line. Certainly Canada's wounded deserved something better.

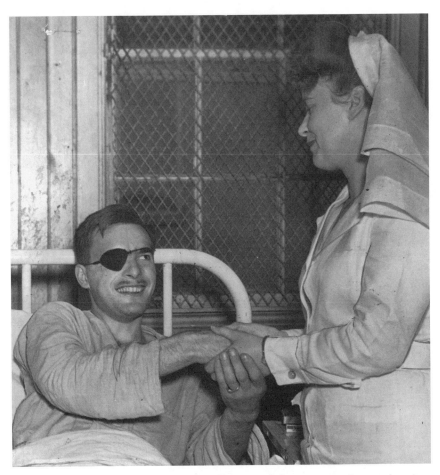

On September 26, 1946, Private Raymond Scott, seen here chatting with nurse Mary Sissen, was getting ready to leave the old Christie Street Hospital. He would become the first patient in the new Sunnybrook Hospital.

The government stood firm. With a world war raging, the lack of both money and building materials precluded any chance of erecting new hospital. Christie Street would just have to do.

The public, however, was adamant in its desire to see a proper veterans' hospital built for Canada's returning heroes. Eventually, through the persistence of local city officials (who convinced the estate of Joseph Kilgour to permit the use of a portion of Sunnybrook Farm, which had been left to the city as a public park by Kilgour's widow, Alice, for hospital purposes) as well as efforts by Lady Eaton, the widow of department store magnate Sir John Craig Eaton, who railed at Premier Mackenzie King every chance she could, the building of a new veterans' hospital was finally approved.

Work commenced in 1943, and the first few patients were transferred from Christie Street to the still-incomplete hospital, soon to be named Sunnybrook, in 1945. Another three years would pass before the facility was officially dedicated by Mackenzie King.

Over the years the mandate of Sunnybrook & Womens' College changed to meet the needs of the time. Today, it has assumed a leadership role in the treatment of cancer, cardiovascular diseases, and a variety of other health problems. It also provides community-based primary and secondary health services as well as serving as one of the country's busiest regional trauma centres.

And while the hospital's prime function has changed over the years, it still attends to the needs of more than five hundred of the nation's aging war heroes. The new Dorothy Macham House continues this noble Sunnybrook tradition.

Another reason that Yarmila and I were pleased to attend the opening is that we knew Dorothy Macham, having met this kindly lady last summer. Dorothy lived nearby and was kind enough to let me park my classic automobile in her garage. By the way, I'll tell the story about how I came to be the owner of that turquoise and white 1955 Pontiac two-door hardtop after I take out a mortgage on the house so I can get enough money to fill its enormous gas tank.

It wasn't until we received the hospital's invitation that we both discovered that our friend Dorothy had been a nursing sister during the Second World War, serving at various front-line aid stations throughout Europe. She was also one of the few females in the Canadian Army to attain the rank of major.

Returning home after the war, Dorothy was appointed Superintendent of Women's College Hospital, a title that was changed in 1970 to Executive Director. She retired in 1975 only to accept the position of Executive Director of West Park Hospital in Weston, where she remained until a second retirement five years later.

In 1980, our friend Dorothy received the Order of Canada.

When Sunnybrook asked the Nursing Sisters Association of Canada to suggest a name for its new veterans' care and research facility, Dorothy Macham was an obvious, and unanimous, choice.

April 29, 2001

At the Crossroads

One of the busiest street intersections in our city is that formed by Queen, King, Roncesvalles, and The Queensway. Up until the late 1950s this foursome was augmented by a fifth, the old Lakeshore Road, which arose from the waterfront to the south on an ancient steel and wood bridge, intersecting the corner about where the small park with the sombre Katyn Memorial (which is dedicated to the fifteen thousand Polish prisoners of war who disappeared from Russian camps in 1940 and the forty-five hundred who were subsequently discovered in mass graves in the Katyn Forest near Smolsensk) is now situated.

That park is located on the site of the old Sunnyside railway station that featured an elevator to transport passengers and luggage to and from the railway platform adjacent to the tracks now used by GO and VIA trains. In the contrasting views accompanying this column we are looking north on Roncesvalles Avenue from Queen. Evident in both photos is the B&G Coffee Shop, which served for many years as a Gray Coach ticket office and has recently been transformed into a McDonald's. Just up the street is the Hotel Edgewater, now a Days Inn.

The history of this landmark is somewhat obscure. Research indicates that it was built sometime between 1937 and 1945 by Messrs. Harris, Dimitrof, and Onazuk, who are listed as owners in the 1945 city directory. Understandably perhaps, the new owners are somewhat reluctant to dwell on the past, choosing to put away that part of the

Roncesvalles Avenue looking north from Queen Street sometime in the early 1940s. Note the War Savings Stamps banners on the hotel.

Same view, 2001. While the Long Branch streetcar no longer stops here, the King car does.

hotel's history and concentrate on its future. Nevertheless, if you have any stories about the Edgewater I'd be glad to read them.

In the older view one of the TTC's "Large" Peter Witt streetcars on the Long Branch route picks up passengers at its eastern terminus (it looped through the nearby Roncesvalles car house) before departing on its run out over the aforementioned bridge, down to Lakeshore Road, and then westerly to the Long Branch loop near the foot of Brown's Line. Witt #2320 was built in 1921 in Montreal and, like most of its mates, was scrapped soon after the Yonge subway opened in March 1954. One "Large" Witt remains in Toronto, its future very much in doubt. Several other Toronto Witt cars (plus many other types of vehicles) can be seen and ridden out at the Halton Country Radial Railway near Rockwood, Ontario.

May 6, 2001

Front and Centre

The old photo that accompanies this column shows something that hasn't been seen for a long, long time. In fact, almost a half-century has gone by since streetcars made their way along Front Street between the North and South St. Lawrence Markets. In this 1953 photo we see a pair of PCC Streamliners eastbound on Front Street just east of Jarvis. The "Private" sign confirms that the cars had been chartered by streetcar buffs and were obviously wandering over track that wasn't normally in use by regular service cars.

Interestingly, both streetcars are "imports" from south of the border purchased by the TTC when many American cities decided to replace their electric vehicles with diesel buses. The car in front (on Front) is an ex-Birmingham, Alabama, PCC, the other is from Cleveland, Ohio. Both had only recently been purchased by the TTC from those cities, which is probably why the buffs had them out on a charter trip.

Incidentally, you too can charter one of the TTC's nicely restored PCC streetcars. They make a great way to celebrate a birthday or a unique venue from which to show off our city to visitors or out-of-town business associates. Details are available from the TTC by calling 416-393-7880. In the background of the 1953 photo we can see the remains of the overhead walkway that connected the North and South Markets for many years until it was demolished a few months after the photo was taken. To the right of the same photo are several buildings that date from the mid-

Front Street looking west to Jarvis Street, 1953.

Same view nearly half a century later.

nineteenth century. The one at the Jarvis Street corner, which was for years a hotel for sailors working the ships that docked just south of Front Street, is now a Golden Griddle restaurant. The building next to it is also original, while the row with the three dormer windows and white sign stretching across the front was torn down many years ago. It has been replaced with a new building that blends in beautifully. The former Turner Wines building is also still there.

May 13, 2001

Foster Father of T.O.

With all the cutbacks and user-pay charges coming out of City Hall these days, it's comforting to know that at least one Toronto politician had the foresight to make sure that the city's kids would be treated to a free picnic each year. And what's even better, that party isn't costing the poor, beleaguered taxpayer one red cent.

Now, if you're thinking of e-mailing your thanks to the person who had the foresight to make sure the kids got their party each year, at no cost to the taxpayer, I'm not sure his address is accessible via the internet. Mayor Foster has been dead for nearly half a century.

Tommy Foster saw the light of day for the first time on July 25, 1852, from the window of the family farmhouse that stood near the corner of the Second Concession West (now Dufferin Street) and the Vaughan Road (so called because that's precisely where it headed, the Township of Vaughan). Eventually, the Foster family moved south into the big city of Toronto and took up residence in a small house in a part of town called Cabbagetown.

As a young man, Tom trained as a butcher and soon had a store of his own on the north side of Queen Street East, right where the Regent Park apartment towers are located today. His shop became one of the most popular in the city, and with his success came financial gain. Tom took most of his money and invested in real estate, and it wasn't long before his hard work made him one of the wealthiest people in Toronto.

To say he was a penny-pincher would do Tom a disservice, for while he was extremely careful how he spent his money, he would frequently share his good fortune with many of the city's less fortunate citizens. And usually, they would never know where that money came from.

In 1891, Foster entered municipal politics and for the next twenty-five years served his adopted city as a ward alderman, a councillor, and, from 1925 to 1927, as its mayor. Throughout his career his business background prompted him to closely scrutinize just how the taxpayers' hard earned money was being spent. This characteristic earned him the title "watchdog of the city treasury."

Thomas Foster, a Toronto mayor who is responsible for the annual Tommy Foster Picnic, which is being presented this year for the fifty-sixth time.

Occasionally, his frugal ways were ridiculed. Like the time he refused to vote in favour of a plan to hire more policemen. Tommy had a better idea, or so he thought. To save the city money, he proposed that any bank that lost money as a result of a hold-up would simply be reimbursed by the city from its own treasury.

Another of his ideas was to have the words "City of Toronto" painted in large letters on all the municipally owned automobiles. That would, he felt, discourage their use for private outings. Perhaps an idea whose time has come again.

Following Foster's retirement from public office, someone calculated that the former mayor's rigid economic standards during his stint at City Hall had saved the city at least $2 million.

Though conservative to the extreme when dealing with money out of city taxpayers' wallets, Foster thought nothing of spending $200,000 from his own on a final resting place for his wife, Elizabeth, and their only daughter, Ruby, who was just ten when she passed away. Situated on a hill northwest of Uxbridge, the stately Foster Mausoleum, looking at a quick glance very much like a miniature Taj Mahal, was dedicated in 1936 and became Tommy's final resting place too following his death on December 10, 1945.

Though Tommy Foster had vanished from the municipal scene, the reading of his will several months later brought one of the city's most flamboyant public servants back into the limelight. In addition to a number of bequests to family members and friends, there were sixteen provisions, which, as Tommy described in his own words, were "to mark my appreciation of my citizenship in Toronto and to place in the way of some citizens or their children opportunities for health and advancement which might otherwise not be theirs."

Varying amounts of money were left for a such things as cancer research, radios for patients in the Hospital for Incurables, seed for Toronto's wild bird population, a wooden flagpole for Central Technical school, cash awards to women who had the largest number of children in four consecutive ten-year periods, and trees to beautify the highways leading into his city.

In addition, he directed that the interest from $100,000 be used for an annual picnic for Toronto children on the condition that "the mayor or a prominent clergyman make a short public address explaining by whom and in what manner the picnic is provided."

This year's Tommy Foster Picnic will be held next Saturday in Rennie Park (foot of Runnymede Road in Swansea). I trust that the terms of the will be met and that in addition to ice cream and cake, the kids will learn something about their benefactor.

May 20, 2001

Planting the Seeds

Just about everyone has heard of the Marx Brothers, the Everley Brothers, the Doobie Brothers, and even the Warner Brothers. Then there are the Big Brothers, Brooks Brothers, Christian Brothers, and the Wright Brothers. And then there's the Rennie Brothers. What, you've never heard of this last trio of siblings? Perhaps that's because the boys were Canadian. And while few today would recognize the names of John, Robert, and Thomas Rennie, there was a time when all three were well known throughout the Dominion.

This was especially so for those engaged in working the soil, since at one time the Rennie Seed Company, of which the boys' father, William, was the founder, was "the largest purveyor of agricultural and horticultural seeds and supplies in Canada."

The Rennie Seed Company was established by the elder Rennie in 1870. The company had extensive experimental and ornamental gardens on both the old Rennie farm in Markham, Ontario, and, after the family's move to the city in 1889, on their newly acquired five-acre farm located on the west bank of Grenadier Pond in the suburban community of Swansea. (The company was purchased by Steele, Briggs in 1961. The latter company was taken over by McKenzie Seeds nine years later.)

Nearby, William Rennie erected for himself and his family a substantial brick house, which was subsequently demolished when the first few houses on Grenadier Heights were erected in the 1920s.

The Rennie Brothers: Thomas, John, and Robert

Rennie had four sons: John, Robert, Thomas, and William Jr. The first three accepted positions in the family seed business, while the latter, William Jr., opted for a missionary's life in far-off Japan. The other three, in addition to working in the thriving Rennie seed business, pursued other interests, each serving either their community or country. As an example of the latter, at the age of nineteen Robert enlisted in the Queen's Own Rifles as a rifleman and after a career of sixty-eight years retired with the rank of major-general. Of special interest is the fact he was in command of the 3rd Battalion, Toronto Regiment when it went overseas in 1915. Robert Rennie was in command of the Queen's Own units during the First World War battles at Ypres, Festubert, and Givenchy. Robert died in 1949 at the age of eighty-seven.

Thomas was also involved with the family business, serving as the company president for many years. He also excelled at curling and for a long period of time was acknowledged as one of the nation's best. Thomas was also a member of the Toronto Harbour Commission, joining the board in 1921 and ultimately serving as its chairman from 1939 to 1947. It was in this capacity that he was honoured by having one of the Toronto Island ferries named after him. Thomas passed away in 1952 at the age of eighty-five.

The third brother, John, who was born in 1865, also worked in the family business serving for many years as its vice-president. Like his younger brother Thomas, John was also an excellent curler. In addition, he also enjoyed the game of golf. It was John Rennie who donated the land on which the present Rennie Park in Swansea is located. As you may recall from last week's column, the fifty-sixth annual Thomas Foster Picnic was held at the park yesterday.

During the dedication ceremony on April 28, 1939, John Rennie described the park, which was 4.5 acres in size and worth $16,000 at the time, as being located on property that had originally been cultivated as a market garden by another pioneer family in Swansea, the Coes, after whom nearby Coe Hill Drive was named. John Rennie also stated that while he wanted his property to be turned over to the children of Swansea to be developed into a playground, he didn't think the taxpayers should have to foot the bill. Rennie would provide the land free of charge because, as he stated at the time, "No further burden of taxation should be imposed on your ratepayers because high taxation will kill the progress of any community." Here, here!

May 27, 2001

Proud, Old Haida

In spite of the weather, last weekend's second annual Doors Open Toronto was a huge success, confirming once again the tremendous interest that Torontonians, as well as hundreds of our neighbours living and working in the surrounding communities, have in our city's built heritage.

While all of the nearly one hundred participants in the event are important, I'd like to make a suggestion for an additional heritage "structure" to be added to the list for next year. I concede that my candidate is somewhat unique in that it's not really a building at all, at least not in the ordinary sense of the word. And opening it to the public, without charge, may prove to be difficult. Nevertheless, my candidate does exhibit a wonderful heritage. What makes it special is that it's the type of heritage born out of love of country and willingness to make the supreme sacrifice to ensure freedom for all Canadians. My candidate is HMCS *Haida*, the proud Royal Canadian Navy destroyer berthed at Ontario Place.

Launched in 1943, *Haida* was one of eight similar Tribal Class vessels built for the RCN in English shipyards. One of her sister ships, HMCS *Athabaskan*, was sunk on April 29, 1944, with the loss of 128 of her officers and men. From the time *Haida* first entered serviced she fought in numerous battles and "showed her stuff" once again during the Korean conflict. Taken off strength in 1963, *Haida* was destined for the wrecker's

HMCS *Haida* as she appeared patrolling the Korean coast in April 1953.

A group of *Haida*'s officers and crew, May 26, 1953.

yard until, almost at the last moment, a group of Torontonians purchased the vessel and towed her to her new home at the foot of York Street, where, in 1965, she was given a new command as naval museum, maritime memorial, and sea cadet training ship. Plans were underway to have her become the centrepiece of a new Servicemen's Memorial Park to be located on the waterfront south of the CNE's Princes' Gates. This concept failed to materialize. Instead, in 1970 *Haida* was moved to her new home at the new provincial showplace Ontario Place, which was to open the following year. HMCS *Haida* continues to be one of Ontario Place's feature attractions.

But *Haida* now faces another battle, a battle as deadly as any she fought in the North Atlantic. If she is to continue reminding us of the sacrifices made by so many to help keep our nation free, *Haida* must undergo a program of extensive, and expensive, repairs. The public is invited to assist the "Friends of *Haida*" with their daunting task by making a financial contribution, large or small. University professor Barry Gough is doing his part by donating all of his earnings from his new book *HMCS* Haida, *Battle Ensign Flying* (Vanwell Publishing Ltd., $50). This wonderful hardcover book is full of informative and entertaining text, rare old photos, and a selection of wartime paintings reproduced in full colour.

June 3, 2001

* On December 11, 2002, HMCS *Haida* was towed from her berth at Ontario Place to the dry dock at Port Weller, where major restoration work was undertaken. On August 28, 2003, *Haida* was towed to her new home in Hamilton Harbour. Two days later official welcoming ceremonies for Canada's newest National Historic Site took place at HMCS Star Naval Reserve Unit, Pier 9. For more information on the vessel check out the website www3.sympatico.ca/hrc/haida.

Move Over Roswell

The other day, while reading about NASA's failed attempt to have one of its experimental jets achieve MACH 7 (seven times the speed of sound or approximately 4,800 miles per hour), I suddenly recalled a time when we here in Canada were on the verge of making aviation history.

To be sure, that was many years ago, near a half-century to be a little more precise. And it wasn't a plane that was to make world aviation history, it was a "flying saucer," and a Canadian-designed and -built "flying saucer" at that.

Perhaps a brief preamble is in order. In 1954, I was in my final year at John Fisher Public School in North Toronto. While others were collecting stamps or hockey cards, I was collecting airplane pictures. That was at a time when all the major aircraft manufacturers would freely send out photos of their products. All I had to do was write and ask. In my collection I had stuff from North American Aviation (F-86 Sabre, F-100 Super Sabre), Boeing (B-47 Stratojet, B-52 Stratofortress), Northrop (F-89 Scorpion), deHavilland (Vampire), Lockheed (F-80 Shooting Star, F-94 Starfire), Republic (F-84 Thunderstreak), and, of course, our own Avro Canada (Jetliner and CF-100 Canuck). The Avro factory was out at Malton Airport, a place I would often ride to on my bike. There I would sit at the end of the runway and watch mesmerized as newly built CF-100s screamed down the runway and up into the clear blue sky.

In 1953, this was a newspaper artist's impression of what Avro Canada's "flying saucer" might look like. The look of the craft was no doubt prompted by similar images in science fiction magazines of the day.

Actual photograph of the new Avrocar.

At the time, my favourite book was *Aircraft of the World,* a copy of which was a Christmas present from my uncle Cookie who also had an interest in planes, having flown twin-engine Wellington bombers during the war. I still have his precious gift, dog-eared as it may be, with many of its pages now held together with transparent tape that isn't transparent anymore. While there were few Canadian aircraft in the book, that would certainly change if what was being secretly planned out at Malton turned out to be a success.

Stories about some sort of revolutionary aircraft being developed at the Avro plant not far from Toronto had been around for months. Nevertheless, when the company finally announced in June, 1954 that it was working on a revolutionary "Flat, Vertical Take-Off Supersonic Gyroplane," a kind of "flying saucer," the aviation world was stunned. Until now, air force officials on both sides of the border had dismissed flying saucers, *aka* "unidentified flying objects," as figments of people's imaginations. In other words, bureaucratically speaking, there was no such thing as a flying saucer!!

For more than half a decade, Canadian and American researchers continued to work on designer Jack Frost's flying saucer, which had been dubbed the Avrocar. In March 1961, after the expenditure of millions of dollars and thousands of man-hours, the project was shelved with the two prototype vehicles assigned to museums south of the border. (There are plans to retrieve at least one of them for a Canadian museum. Perhaps Sheila can help.) A little more than a year later, Avro Canada, which had fostered two other revolutionary aircraft that were "shot down," the Jetliner and Arrow, was no more.

The decision to abandon the Avro flying saucer project prompts several questions. Was it able to take off vertically? Sort of. Did it reach supersonic speeds? Definitely not. Did it make the revised edition of *Aircraft of the World?* Not even as a footnote. Therefore, the Avrocar must have been a failure. Well, in the strictest sense, perhaps it was. But a more complete answer would have to acknowledge that the Avrocar was well ahead of its time and that many of the engineering concepts it pioneered would be used in the future development of other forms of land, sea, and air transportation. To learn the full story of this Canadian dream pick up a copy of Bill Zuk's new book *Avrocar: Canada's Flying Saucer, the Story of Avro Canada's Secret Projects.*

Looking for a reason to party tomorrow? Why not stop by the Royal York Hotel and toast this Toronto landmark as she celebrates her seventy-second birthday. It was on June 11, 1929, that the then Governor General of Canada, Lord Willington, officially opened the 1,200-room, 27-storey hotel, at the time the largest and most modern in the country. The cost of construction was $18 million. So popular was the new hotel that several additions were made, including a 400-room, 17-storey structure that opened in early 1959. Its cost? $15 million. Incidentally, if you're going to phone the hotel for a room or restaurant reservation you won't find the number under Royal York. Nope, you have to look under Fairmont, the hotel's official name being the Fairmont Royal York. Incidentally, here's a little Royal York, oops Fairmont Royal York trivia for your next party. Who was the first guest to sign the room register at the new hotel? Mrs. Kenneth Mackenzie of Winnipeg.

The Royal York new C.P.R. Hotel, Toronto, Canada.

Whoever drew this likeness of the recently announced Royal York Hotel for a new postcard, he (or she) obviously didn't work from the architect's final drawings.

June 10, 2001

Forever Yonge

Happy Birthday to you,
Happy Birthday to you,
Happy Birthday Sir George,
Happy Birthday to You.

Last week we celebrated the Royal York, oops Fairmont Royal York Hotel's seventy-second birthday. This week we have another reason to party. Tomorrow is the birthday of someone whose name has become known all over town. Actually, from top to bottom.

And who might that be?

Sir George Yonge, the man for whom our main drag, as well as the main drags of many communities from here to the Ontario-Minnesota border, was named. Unfortunately, George will be unable to respond to our good wishes since he passed away 189 years ago. Nevertheless, had he survived his death, tomorrow would have been his 269th birthday. Interestingly, George never saw any of the street signs on which his name was inscribed, or anything else here in North America for that matter. In fact, his connection with our community was only from a distance.

Sir George was an acquaintance of John Graves Simcoe, the province's first lieutenant governor and the founder of our city, by virtue of the fact that Yonge represented the Devonshire borough of Honiton in the British parliament. Simcoe's estate, Wolford Lodge, was located

74

in Honiton. In addition, the two were colleagues in government for a very brief time during Simcoe's tenure as the representative of the nearby Cornish borough of St. Mawes.

More important was the fact that at the very time Simcoe was busy trying to get his new province up and running in the late 1790s, Yonge was (as they called it

Tomorrow's birthday boy, Sir George Yonge (1732–1812), after whom Yonge Street is named.

Southwest corner of Yonge and Front streets. The Customs House was arguably the stateliest of all the buildings erected on Yonge Street. Constructed in 1876, it survived the Great Fire of 1904 only to be wantonly converted to rubble fifteen years later.

Same view, 2001.

back then) the Secretary at War, an extremely prestigious position in the cabinet of King (King Street) George III. Simcoe recognized how important having acquaintances in high places was to the future development of his little town. Naming a street wasn't a bad way to get Yonge's attention. However, according to Henry Scadding, Toronto's pre-eminent historian, the main reason for Simcoe naming one of the two most important thoroughfares in the new province Yonge (the other was Dundas Street) then taking it a step further by adding the term *street* (a word derived from the Latin *strada* and descriptive of a well constructed public way usually paved with stone — in other words the "state of the art" in road construction) was because of Sir George's expertise in both the history and techniques associated with Roman road building.

Simcoe believed that it would add prestige to his new town to have one of the new province's main arteries named in honour of such an expert. And so Yonge it was, and is.

June 17, 2001

25 Years and Counting

While it's true that next Tuesday our very own CN Tower will celebrate the twenty-fifth anniversary of its official opening (a quarter of a century, can you believe it?), what's even more fascinating is the fact that the plan to build the tower was first presented publicly almost a decade earlier.

In another strange twist, had the promoters of what was to be known as Metropolitan Centre (of which the tower was to be a key element) been able to look into the future, there's every possibility that the CN Tower wouldn't have been built at all.

The Metropolitan Centre project, which was first announced in 1966, was described at the time as the greatest urban redevelopment scheme ever proposed for a North American city.

Over time, it was said, the project would result in the redevelopment of the 187 acres of under-utilized property bounded by Yonge Street on the east, Bathurst Street on the west, the Gardiner Expressway to the south, and Front Street to the north. Added to this almost rectangular parcel was a smaller tract of land on the north boundary that stretched as far north as King Street.

According to media stories written in the fall of 1967, by the time this massive project was completed some fifteen to twenty years in the future, a network of office towers, shopping malls, parks, plazas, townhouses, and apartments (there was no mention of condominiums back

This model of the proposed Metropolitan Centre project shows a communications tower that differs greatly from the tower that was actually built and opened to the public twenty-five years ago this year.

then) would cover the site. In addition, Metropolitan Centre would have an ultra-efficient transportation facility to serve inter-city buses and trains. Later plans listed a convention centre, hotels, and a new Massey Hall.

On the section of land reaching from the main parcel northward to King, and flanked on either side by John and Simcoe streets, a new headquarters for the CBC would be built. As an added incentive for the corporation to abandon its plans to move to a site near Eglinton

Avenue and Don Mills Road the broadcast centre would have a fifteen-hundred-foot broadcasting tower.

(Ultimately, this tower would be replaced by the present CN Tower, which is used by a wide array of communications and broadcasting businesses.) The announcement, made on September 12, 1967, was the first public mention of a tower for downtown Toronto.

Participants in the Metropolitan Centre project, a term that was eventually simplified to Metro Centre, were varied with the main pair being the powerful CN and CP railways. In fact, it was the move of their age-old freight yards from Toronto's waterfront to new sites in Vaughan and Markham, respectively, that would be the catalyst behind the project.

Over the next few months officials valiantly predicted that construction of Metro Centre would soon be underway. "Spring Start on Super Centre" crowed the December 17, 1968, edition of the *Toronto Telegram*. Nothing happened. In a November 22, 1971, *Globe and Mail* story then Alderman John Sewell, the most vocal opponent of the

A key player in the construction of the CN Tower was Olga, a giant Sikorsky Skycrane helicopter that helped top off the remarkable structure in April 1975. Nearly two decades later Olga is still hard at work. Here Toronto *Sunday Sun* reader Robert Ough poses with her during a refuelling stop deep in the interior of British Columbia.

project, stated the "Metro Centre is about to take off into the financial and construction arms of Toronto." Again, nothing happened.

Though it was initially greeted with great enthusiasm, flaws in the project soon began to appear that led to a series of postponements. One of the most serious flaws had to do with access to and from the site by public transit. Both the municipality and TTC steadfastly refused to extend the Yonge/University subway south from Union Station or construct the three stations (Esplanade East, Queen's Quay, and Esplanade West) deemed necessary to serve the sprawling project. The cost of such additions, at least $50 million, was just too much for the taxpayers to absorb. (As a bit of an aside, the new 5-station, 2.8-mile Sheppard subway now under construction is budgeted at $875 million.)

There were numerous other flies in the ointment, not the least of which was Metro Centre's insistence that the city's grand old Union Station had no place in its plans for a transportation centre. It would have to come down, an ultimatum that did not rest lightly with many Torontonians. The suggestion that the Great Hall could be preserved for some unidentified purpose did nothing to serve the preservationists.

There were many other roadblocks, but suffice it to say it was the city's demand that Union Station be retained that ultimately burst the Metro Centre bubble. However, when the Metro Centre officials walked away from the project, the communications tower, which had now been redesigned (the original three-legged structure was now solid with a hollow core and its height had increased from a mere 1,500 feet to a world record 1,815 feet 6 inches), was already on its way skyward. Undaunted, work on what had been renamed the C(anadian) N(ational) Tower (the other railway had walked away from the project) went ahead, and on June 26, 1976, "the world's tallest free-standing structure," complete with observation decks, restaurant, and array of communications devices, as first proposed, was officially opened to an amazed public.

June 24, 2001

Toronto's Capital Idea

Happy Canada Day!!

Once again happy crowds will gather on Parliament Hill in the nation's capital to wish our marvellous country another happy birthday. But had good Queen Victoria not poked her royal nose into the young nation's business, it's quite possible that those same crowds would be converging on Toronto and not Ottawa to celebrate the nation's birthday. Just imagine, had things gone differently, when Regis asked the question, "Which of the following cities is the capital of Canada — Kingston, Montreal, Quebec, or Toronto?" the answer might have been the last.

Actually, it could have been any of the four. To find out why Ottawa is our nation's capital we have to go back to the early 1840s when Canada was merely a province in British North America. It had been formed as a result of the passage in 1840 of something called the Act of Union. This legislation joined together as one entity the former provinces of Upper Canada and Lower Canada (now known as Ontario and Quebec, respectively). This new province was given the name Canada.

It then became necessary to select a site where the province of Canada's governing body could meet. Kingston, Upper Canada, was the first choice, and it served as the capital of the new province until May 10, 1844.

These photos show a trio of the buildings that were around when our country was born on July 1, 1867. Two of them, and a portion of the third, still stand. (Above) Work on the Don Jail began in 1858 and took many years to complete, the structure having been partially destroyed by fire while still under construction. Its first "guests" arrived in 1864, three years before the birth of Canada. (Right) The centre portion of today's South St. Lawrence Market was constructed as part of Toronto's first purpose-built city hall.

To even things up (politically) the capital was relocated to Montreal for the next five years. This bouncing around continued, with Toronto serving as the third capital from November 14, 1849, until September 22, 1851. Then it was back east again, with Quebec

City holding the title for the next four years. Toronto became the capital once again, this time from October 20, 1855, until September 24, 1859. Then back to Quebec City for the next six years.

In an attempt to end this costly, inefficient jockeying of provincial capital cities hither and thither, it was proposed in 1857 that whichever communities in the province wanted to be the site of the permanent capital put it in writing. Good Queen Victoria, everybody's favourite, would have the final say.

Toronto made its pitch in a memorandum dated February 27, 1858. It contained comments put forward by a "Select Committee of the Common Council of the City of Toronto." To paraphrase the rambling report, Toronto had it all over all others in the running when it came to wealth, business, commerce, and military defensibility. Some of the statements made by the committee members to support their conclusions would be unacceptable today. For instance, it was suggested that Protestants, who were more prevalent in Toronto than in either Montreal or Quebec City, weren't in church as much as the Catholics were so they (the Protestants) could pay more attention to business matters.

The Jolly Miller Tavern on Yonge Street was well north of Bloor Street, the city's northernmost boundary in 1867. In that same year the York Mills Hotel (as it was then known) was celebrating its tenth anniversary.

Another statement in the Toronto report claimed that "the French race" was distinguished by a "calm contentment ... [that led to a] ... feeble attachment of the habitants to the bustle and business even of their own capitals."

And you think Mel put his foot in it.

Whether these and other claims in the document were true really didn't matter, for on December 31, 1857, Queen Victoria ruled that Ottawa was to be her choice as the site of the Province of Canada's permanent capital. Her proclamation was to take effect on October 20, 1865.

On July 1, 1867, the Province of Canada resolved itself into two new provinces, Ontario and Quebec, which were confederated with the two existing provinces of New Brunswick and Nova Scotia to form the new Dominion of Canada. Ottawa then gained a new role. It was now the new nation's capital city, an honour that, except for Queen Victoria's decision a decade earlier, might have been Toronto's.

July 1, 2001

* The Jolly Miller Tavern recently reopened as The Miller restaurant.

On a Pioneer Quest

What do the following names conjure up for you: Alice, Carol, Dolly, Edna, Florence, and Gilda? To some of you guys out there, perhaps they're the names of some of the girls from your high school or college days. However, if I add one more name to the list, Hazel, perhaps the events associated with this collection will become clear. That's right, these names identify the seven hurricanes that ravaged various parts of North America back in 1954.

Of particular interest to Ontarians was the last named storm in that list. Hazel was born on October 5, 1954, in the Caribbean Sea. A few days later, after battering the island of Haiti and killing nearly one thousand people, Hazel made landfall near the state line between North and South Carolina. From there the storm roared northward, pummelling Washington, D.C. Then, instead of veering to the northeast as most ordinary storms were supposed to do, Hazel maintained a northerly course, causing flooding and extensive damage in western Pennsylvania and New York state. Hazel then did the unthinkable: she took dead aim at southern Ontario, and more specifically Toronto.

As a result of several weeks of rain, the ground in and around our city was saturated, so when Hazel arrived early in the evening of Friday, October 15, her torrential downpour had nowhere to go but into the nearby rivers and creeks. Now Toronto and the surrounding communities really had a problem. It wasn't long before both the Rouge and the

These three buildings (left to right: the second Stong house, 1832; the first Stong house, 1816; and the Stong grain barn, 1825) form the nucleus of today's Black Creek Pioneer Village.

The Halfway House was originally at the northwest corner of Kingston and Midland roads in Scarborough. Halfway House was so named because it was halfway between Toronto's St. Lawrence Hall and the Dunbarton post office (near Whitby). The house was rescued from demolition and moved to Pioneer Village, where it reopened in 1967.

Don were overflowing their banks. But it was the seething waters of the usually peaceful Mimico Creek and Humber River that were to cause the most serious problems.

In fact, by the time the storm had dissipated a few hours later millions in property damage had been done. Even worse was the number of dead. More than eighty citizens had lost their lives during Hazel's brief visit.

As devastating as Hazel may have been, her unexpected arrival in southern Ontario forty-seven years ago is the very reason why we have one of the city's most interesting attractions, Black Creek Pioneer Village.

Just days after Hazel's visit, government officials met to discuss how best to prevent, or at the very least diminish, the impact that a similar disaster would have on the newly created Municipality of Metropolitan Toronto. One of the first things they decided on was that no longer would approval be given to construct residences on flood-prone parcels of land.

With that ruling in place, the Humber Valley Conservation Authority, under whose jurisdiction the death-dealing Humber River fell, determined that the fourteen acres at the northwest corner of Steeles Avenue and Jane Street through which one of the Humber's tributaries, Black Creek, flowed was no place for housing —and to preclude that possibility they went ahead and purchased the land.

Interestingly, on that property stood the old Dalziel (pronounced Dee-el) Barn, so named for the pioneer Dalziel family that had immigrated to the area from Scotland in the early 1800s. With great foresight, especially at a time in our city's history when newer always meant better, the authority agreed to keep and restore the old barn. It eventually became the cornerstone of the new Dalziel Pioneer Park.

One of the park's benefactors was a lady who had been born nearby and had spent much of her childhood living in a house on the Dalziel property. Back then her name was Florence Nightingale Graham. As the years went by the world got to know her better as Elizabeth Arden.

In early 1957 the Humber River Conservation Authority merged with several other local authorities to form the Metro Toronto and Region Conservation Authority (now simply the Toronto and Region Conservation Authority). The next year the little pioneer park expanded with the acquisition of the nearby Stong property. Not only had the park grown in size, it now had a grand total of four buildings.

Later that same year saw the move of the Burwick House from Woodbridge to the park site. This 1884 "gentleman's house" was the first of several "newcomers" to the site.

Today, what we now know as Black Creek Pioneer Village has a treasure trove of nearly fifty structures we all can still admire. And it's all thanks to that mean old Hurricane Hazel.

July 8, 2001

TTC Treasures on Display

Ever wonder where old Toronto streetcars go when they're no longer needed? It wasn't that long ago that many were simply sold to scrap dealers who would take cutting torches to the vehicles, carving them into metal pieces of various shapes and sizes, which would then be sold by the pound to a variety of customers.

Every once in a while an American streetcar museum would put in an offer to buy an old car, and if its bid was successful the car would soon be on its way to a new home south of the border. Toronto's transportation heritage was slowly, but surely, slipping away.

It wasn't until 1953 that a group of dedicated streetcar "buffs" finally decided to do something about preserving what little was left of the city's dwindling transit heritage. As a result of their collective concerns, those same buffs established the Ontario Electric Railway Association. Initially, its mandate was simply to preserve examples of Toronto's various types of streetcars. That modest mandate changed over the years, and now, in addition to numerous streetcars, the association's collection features a couple of the original Yonge subway cars, seven city trolley coaches, plus an assortment of unwanted electric transit vehicles from other municipalities and jurisdictions. There are also all sorts of ancient railway work equipment and even a gasoline bus or two.

While the association members were busy finding treasures to add to the organization's roster (some vehicles were being used as chicken

Wooden TTC streetcar #1326 on Front Street in front of the Royal York Hotel, March 30, 1952. Note the use of wooden planking on Front Street as subway construction progresses, slowly. The Yonge subway would open exactly three years after this picture was taken.

Visitors can still ride old #1326 at the Halton County Radial Railway Museum. Its companion in this photo is #55, which was built in 1915 and also operated on Toronto streets. It was also saved from destruction by the museum members.

coops or country residences), they also wanted to put their discoveries on display for all to see. Actually, it was more than that. They wanted people young and old to experience the thrill of riding on board these gems from the past.

To that end, the association acquired land near Rockwood, Ontario, (not far from Guelph) and went about re-laying track on a section of an abandoned right-of-way once used by the big radial cars of the Toronto Suburban Railway as they shuttled their way between west Toronto to Guelph. Before long a powerhouse was in place (streetcars work well without gasoline, but aren't worth a darn without electricity, the 600-volt direct current kind), overhead wires were strung, car barns were built, and, on June 25, 1972, the first paying passengers had the ride of their lives on the streetcars of the newly opened Halton County Radial Railway Museum.

One of the first streetcars to be rescued was old #1326. This vehicle was built in 1910 by the TTC's forerunner, the Toronto Railway Company (TRC) in its shop on Front Street East near Sherbourne. When the privately owned TRC was superseded by the new municipally owned Toronto Transportation Commission eighty years ago (watch for a special TTC birthday event early this coming September) old #1326 became part of the TTC fleet of cars joining other TRC cars and the TTC's new Peter Witts. It remained in service for the next thirty years.

When it was finally retired, #1326, the commission's last wooden streetcar, received special recognition in a parade that wound its way through downtown Toronto on March 30, 1952. It was accompanied by one of the then modern upstarts, the PCC car, which has also been retired — that is, except for #4500 and #4549, which are available for charter from the TTC (call 416-393-7880 for details).

A special treat is in store out at the museum on July 22 for those who enjoy old streetcars as well as old automobiles. On that day the museum will hold its annual custom and classic car show. Participants who drive their ancient chariots out to the museum will be given reduced rate admission. No pre-registration is necessary.

The Halton County Radial Railway is on the Guelph Line (exit 312) ten miles north of Highway 401. For additional details see the museum's web site, www.hcry.org, or phone 519-856-1399.

July 15, 2001

Country Roads Now
Busy Scarborough Intersection

Those who frequent the busy Eglinton Avenue/Victoria Park part of our city will find it hard, no impossible, to comprehend that there was a time not that long ago when this part of the world was nothing but rolling farmland with the two aforementioned streets appearing through the long grass as nothing but narrow, dirt-covered pathways.

To be sure, these paths were somewhat different in appearance, Eglinton being a wider dirt-covered path than Victoria Park (or, as the thoroughfare was called back then, O'Connor Drive). It was simply an extension of a recently constructed street that extended out into the countryside from the city to make it easier to get to and from the heretofore almost unreachable property of the well-known founder of the Laura Secord chocolate enterprise, Frank O'Connor. The wealthy Senator O'Connor just happened to be friendly with all good Liberals and a particular favourite of Prime Minister Mackenzie King. Enough said.

With the outbreak of the Second World War, the pastoral setting of this part of Scarborough Township would soon change. In the early part of the conflict things were not going well for the Allies. One of the most serious problems facing the fighting men was the lack of a sure and uninterrupted source of weaponry and the associated ammunition, in the form of bombs, bullets, and shells, needed to get the job done.

A major step to alleviate this problem was a commitment made by the Canadian government to erect a modern fuse plant (fuses being a major component of artillery shells that detonated the shell automatically, whether there was a direct hit or not — no fuse, no boom). The site selected for this particular plant, known officially as "Project 24," was on a flat, grassy field on the south side of Eglinton Avenue, east of O'Connor Drive in the Township of Scarborough. The exact location of the almost 360-acre property was on "Lots 31, 32 and 33, Concession C, Scarboro Township," running 4,500 feet south from Eglinton and bounded on the east and west, respectively, by the modern Warden and Birchmount avenues.

The official documents were signed in early 1941, and soon the company that was selected to erect and operate the plant, the General Engineering Company (known locally as GECO, a construction company originally established in 1903 in Utah and a highly experienced organization that had already erected several buildings for the RCAF), was on the scene. The huge complex, consisting of 172 buildings, large and small, most of which were interconnected by a labyrinth of underground tunnels, was completed by the end of 1941.

Soon the first of more than six thousand employees, mostly women and mostly from the nearby City of Toronto, began arriving, and it was-

Toronto-born Mary Pickford, "America's Sweetheart" and the world's first true motion picture star, gave morale a tremendous boost when she visited the GECO plant in 1943.

n't long before the first shipment of the much needed fuses was being loaded on rail cars lined up in great numbers on nearby spur lines. By the end of the war the GECO plant had turned out more than 256 million fuses for the Allied war effort.

Much of the preceding information came to me thanks to Warren Evans, whom I met after he had read my original GECO story in the *Sunday Sun* many years ago. Warren knew the GECO story well, but not as an employee of the war plant. He was one of many who, because of the city's severe post-war housing shortage, became a member of the unique GECO residential community that occupied the factory buildings, a community that lasted until the area was redeveloped in the 1950s by township officials under the supervision of Scarborough's crusty, but visionary, Reeve Oliver Crockford.

Warren has written a book that deals with his experiences as a child of GECO. In the author's own words, his new book documents "an extraordinary experience in my youth which just had to be penned to paper ... an ageless story for all ages with no geographical of cultural boundaries!"

Goldfinches of GECO (softcover, 679 pages, $38.95 plus $5 shipping) is available from the author. Send cheques (made out to Warren Evans) to GECO, P.O. Box 631, Pickering, ON, L1V 3T3.

July 22, 2001

Toronto's Finest Walkin' the Beat through History

One of Toronto Police Services busiest stations is 51 Division on Regent Street. In the scheme of things, this facility, which serves the east central part of the city from Rosedale down to the harbour, is quite an "ancient" structure, having opened way back in 1954.

Interestingly, even in those days critics were complaining that the amount of money spent on the new station was nothing short of scandalous.

When it opened, today's 51 Division was identified as No.4 and was built to replace an even older No.4 that had served the surrounding community for decades. This 1880s structure stood just around the corner, on the south side of Dundas just east of the Parliament Street corner. Jack Webster, who recently retired as Honourary Curator of the Police Museum (a place well worth visiting), recalls a time when officers assigned to No. 4 would nail their lunch bags to the ceiling to keep the contents out of the reach of the station's rat population.

In 1957, the thirteen police forces that existed in Metropolitan Toronto were joined into one entity. A few years later the District system was established to improve the efficiency of the force, and with that No.4 became 51 Division in 5 District.

Since then 51 Division has worked out of the Regent Street facility. In a few years, however, 51 be "serving and protecting" from its new home at the northeast corner of Front and Parliament streets.

Facing top: Aerial view taken in the early 1950s looking down on the Front/Parliament corner. The old Consumers' Gas purification building is evident, as are some of the other facilities that made up Consumers' Gas Station "A."

Above: The 1899 gas purification building as it looks today.

Below: The new 51 Division as it will look incorporating part of the 1899 structure.

And to show just how far we've progressed in our attempts to pre-serve what little we have from an earlier Toronto, a portion of the old Consumers' Gas building that has stood on the corner since 1899 will be incorporated into the overall design.

Actual work on the project will commence later this summer and architect Michael Moxom anticipates that the new 51 Division will be in business late next year or early in 2003. The three images that accompany this article illustrate the transformation that this old city street corner will soon undergo.

Special thanks to Insp. Mike Sale for his help in piecing together 51 Division's history.

July 29, 2001

* The new 51 Division was officially opened on June 15, 2004.

Celebrating Simcoe

It's often been said that Canadians are the most reluctant people on the planet to wave their own flag. Seldom do we let the rest of the world know about our nation's many achievements. To be perfectly honest, most Canadians don't even know what those achievements are.

And when it comes to recognizing those who have helped make the place where we live great, we're even more hesitant to tell the story. A case in point: most Ontarians continue to refer to tomorrow's holiday by the nondescript phrase "Civic Holiday." I often wonder how many of them think the day simply honours a model of Japanese car?

Back in 1969, Toronto mayor William Dennison and his council tried to do something nationalistic by announcing that from henceforth the day would be known as Simcoe Day, thereby honouring John Graves Simcoe, the man who, in 1792, founded a community that has grown into the present City of Toronto and, of equal importance, who was first to hold the position of lieutenant-governor of the Province of Upper Canada (renamed Ontario in 1867).

To be sure Simcoe had his faults. Some of the things he said and did would be unacceptable today. But in the context of his time, most of his actions can be justified. For instance, the granting of large parcels of land to his friends in high places would, in this day and age, no doubt result in an official investigation. But back then, how else could he get the people so necessary to the successful beginnings of his new

Courtesy the Toronto Sun Archives

Work nears completion on the city's new Lord Simcoe Hotel at the northeast corner of University and King. The place lasted a mere twenty-two years and then, *poof*, it, like John Simcoe himself, was history.

town and province to come and live in what was not much more than an impenetrable forest?

While the term Simcoe Day has been accepted in the old City of Toronto as well as in the former Borough of East York, elsewhere in the "new" city, and throughout most of the rest of the province as well, the term just hasn't caught on.

That's not to say there isn't any recognition out there. To the north we have Simcoe County and to the west, the pretty little Town of Simcoe. And there are Simcoe streets in several Ontario communities. Wait a minute, you cry. What about the most obvious Simcoe? You know, the one a few miles up the 400, Lake Simcoe? While the county, town, and streets were certainly named in recognition of our first lieutenant-governor, truth is the lake was actually named by Simcoe to honour his father.

Locally, we have John and Simcoe streets (we had a Graves, but that vanished years ago with the renaming of Spadina south of King). And we have Simcoe Place on Front Street near the CBC building. And for a few years we even had a hotel that tried to recognize the city's founder.

Courtesy the *Toronto Sun* Archives

A.V. Potter, head of Eaton's design department, with the painting of Simcoe that was on view in his (sort of) namesake hotel.

Unfortunately, the management went a little too far. They named the new place, which opened at the northeast corner of King and University on May 15, 1957, the Lord Simcoe Hotel. Now, Simcoe may have been a lot of things, but a lord he wasn't.

Many experts believe he should have been awarded that honour and, in fact, some references indicate that a peerage was actually on the way. The idea was set aside following Simcoe's untimely death at the age of just forty-nine on October 26, 1806.

Oh, and that hotel. For messing with history it was demolished just twenty-two years after it opened. Not really — the land on which it sat was just too valuable. Room rates couldn't be boosted high enough to make the business a financial success, so down it came. The corporate headquarters of Sun Life of Canada now sits on the corner.

August 5, 2001

One More Time Around

Recently, my wife and I spent a pleasant afternoon roaming the back roads of the beautiful Niagara Peninsula. Our ultimate destination was the pretty little community of Port Dalhousie (which became part of St. Catharines in 1961) and the Port Mansion Theatre Restaurant, at one time known as the Union Hotel, where many of the crew members working the ships traversing the old Welland Canal would eat and sleep. The beautifully restored building overlooks Lake Ontario, the remnants of that first canal, and a restored carousel that was built by the Charles Looff Company sometime in the late 1890s or early 1900s.

Before dinner and the show, we had to have several spins on that carousel, which still operates with the aid of one of those heavy Westinghouse controllers that appears to have been borrowed from an old streetcar. This leads me to believe that the carousel did, in fact, come from Toronto's Scarboro Beach amusement park, a typical old-fashioned "trolley park" started by the TTC's forerunner, the Toronto Railway Company. The place was closed in 1925, and houses soon stood where there once were rides and side show tents. One of those rides, the carousel, eventually made it to Port Dalhousie's Lakeside Park where it was lovingly restored and continues to delight young and old at a nickel a ride.

In fact, I could almost hear the laughter and yells of the thousands of Torontonians that would arrive here each summer season from the

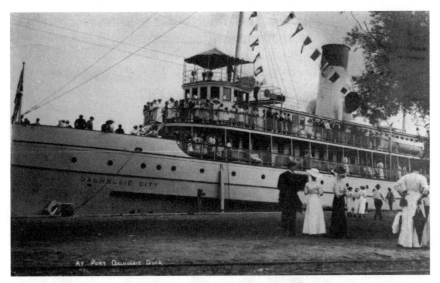

Fun seekers from Toronto arrive at Lakeside Park's Port Dalhousie dock on board the steamer *Dalhousie City, circa* 1920.

steamy city on the other side of the lake on board one of the ancient lake steamers: *Garden City, Lakeside, Northumberland,* or *Dalhousie City.* That pilgrimage ended in 1950 when the automobile took over and the last of the lake boats was removed from service.

An indispensable feature of our annual Canadian National Exhibition is Warriors' Day and its associated parade. The first Warrior's Day was held eighty years ago this year when those in charge agreed that rather than a holding a few informal events throughout the city to mark the anniversary of the end of the Great War, a special Warrior's Day would be held during the CNE. The main feature of this day would be a colourful parade in which all military service veterans would be invited to participate. The first official Warrior's Day was held in 1921, at which time the Governor General of the day, Baron Byng of Vimy, addressed the more than twelve thousand veterans of the South African and First World Wars who had gathered on the Exhibition Grounds to honour fallen comrades and rejoice in their victories.

To celebrate the eightieth anniversary of Warriors' Day, a blue and gold Ontario Heritage Foundation commemorative plaque will be unveiled next Saturday. The plaque will be erected adjacent to the Princes' Gates, through which countless thousands of veterans have paraded each Warriors' Day since the royal brothers, princes Edward and George, dedicated the imposing structure on August 30, 1927. A musical finale, directed by Major Gino Falconi and dedicated to Canada's war veterans, will be featured in the Coliseum following the parade.

One of the regiments that has participated in each and every Warriors' Day since the day's inception eighty years ago is our famous 48th Highlanders of Canada. In fact, the 48th is thirty years older than Warriors' Day, having been established here in Toronto in 1891. To hon-

Members of the 48th Highlanders of Canada parade through the Princes' Gates in the fall of 1939. This famous regiment was a regular participant in the CNE's annual Warriors' Day Parade.

our the regiment's 110 years of service to our nation George (Geordie) Beal has written *Family of Volunteers, an Illustrated History of the 48th Highlanders of Canada*. Published by the Robin Brass Studio, the book is a valuable addition to any proud Canadian's library.

August 12, 2001

Sub Lore Lives On

When I first began collecting photographs of "old" Toronto some thirty years ago one of the first ones I added to my collection was a view taken from the roof of the then new Toronto Harbour Commission Building on the city's waterfront, which showed the German submarine UC-97 being "paraded" through Toronto Harbour. This event occurred in the summer of 1919, and with the Great War still fresh in everyone's memory the visit was covered in the city's many daily newspapers.

The captured sub was described as an American "war prize" and an example of the type of vicious weapon the enemy would use to win the war at any cost. She was on her way to a naval station in Chicago with side trips to various Great Lake ports, including Toronto, to "show the colours."

That was it, that was all I knew about the UC-97. Then along came the Internet.

One day while looking for something totally different on the net, I entered in Google's search field the term "UC-97." To my amazement, up popped that entire history of what was described in 1919 as the enemy's "fiercesome war boat." Her keel had been laid in a Hamburg, Germany, shipyard in late 1917 and launched in March 1918. The Armistice was signed before UC-97 had completed her sea trials, and the vessel was never commissioned. She never

105

The captured German submarine UC-97 moored in front of the newly constructed Toronto Harbour Commission building, June 10, 1919. The once-feared vessel now rests on the bottom of Lake Michigan.

fired a torpedo, never laid a mine, but for the Americans, UC-97 was, nevertheless, a war trophy.

Actually, the UC-97 would go on to enter the history books for another, more intriguing, reason.

On July 24, 1915, the steamer *Eastland*, one of Chicago's most popular pleasure steamers, was loading passengers at her dock prior to a day excursion to Michigan City, Indiana. The happy crowds still waiting in line feared the ship would leave without them and began to rush the gangplank. The vessel started to list towards the dock and in an instant turned over, throwing hundreds into the river and trapping hundreds more inside. The final death toll was 844, all but three being crew members. Like the sinking of our *Empress of Ireland* in the St. Lawrence River earlier that same year, the number of passengers that died in the *Eastland* disaster exceeded the number of *Titanic* passengers who had perished three years before. The sinking of the *Eastland* remains the worst disaster in Great Lakes history.

And here's the kicker. Following the tragedy, the *Eastland* was raised and converted into a naval training ship known as the USS *Wilmette*. As part of her gunnery exercises, she fired on a number of vessels, including the captured UC-97. It was on June 17, 1921, that the once-proud German submarine, after several direct hits from the

Wilmette's guns, went to the bottom of Lake Michigan, where she rests to this day.

To learn more about the *Eastland* and the UC-97 contact the Eastland Disaster Historical Society, PO Box 2013, Arlington Heights, Illinois 60006-2013.

August 19, 2001

New Life from Liberty

Visitors to this year's CNE will probably not notice it, but one of Exhibition Place's most attractive structures is undergoing a marvellous rebirth. Plans by the Liberty Entertainment Group to give new life to the former Ontario Government Building (OGB) at the west end of the grounds are especially welcome when one looks at the list of CNE structures that have succumbed to flames or, worse still, to the seemingly unending work of the city's all-too-busy wrecking crews.

Over the fair's 123 years, the fire fiend has been a frequent visitor. Flames have devoured the Crystal Palace, the Manufacturers' Building, the old Grandstand, the International Building (serving as the Spanish Pavilion), and the Railway (Music) Building. Only the last was resurrected. Other CNE structures, such as the Electrical and Engineering Building, the Art Gallery, General Exhibits, and Graphic Arts buildings, the Shell (Bulova) Tower, and even the popular Flyer roller coaster, were simply pulled down.

In fact, even the Ontario Government Building, which was erected over a nine-month period in late 1925/1926 to the design of the prominent Toronto architectural firm of Chapman and Oxley (creators of Havergal College on Avenue Road, the Northern Ontario Building at Bay and Adelaide streets and the CNE's Princes' Gates) faced an uncertain future following a fire that destroyed the Spanish Pavilion in August of 1974.

Ontario Premier George H. Ferguson addresses the assembled multitude as the new Ontario Government Building is officially opened on August 28, 1926.

The attractive building was a favourite subject for souvenir postcards, such as this one published in the late 1920s.

The ruins were still smouldering when plans surfaced that would have seen Dufferin Street extended south, through the site, to intersect with Lake Shore Boulevard. That would eliminate the jog just south of the Dufferin Gate and, not coincidentally, put the Ontario Government

One of my favourite memories of my visits to the Ontario Government Building as a kid was seeing Paul Bunyan and his giant blue ox, Babe, both created out of papier maché.

Building outside the CNE Grounds. The ancient building's usefulness would have been jeopardized, its fate sealed.

Fortunately, like many of the plans developed for Exhibition Place over the years, the suggestion to extend the street was never acted on and the OGB struggled on. Many will remember the building best when it was the showplace for goods manufactured in Ontario complete with displays of new provincial highway projects, or as the place where we could see, in person, such "wild beasts" as raccoons, foxes, and skunks captured and brought to the city folk from some of the wondrous provincial forests.

The Ontario government abandoned the building in 1971, just months after the opening of Ontario Place across the street. Two years later the old structure became home to the Calgary Corral. Then, from 1974 to 1986, it was the Carlsberg Pavilion (remember Jack Fraser's magnificent horses out front?) and in 1987 to 1988 the Carling O'Keefe Pavilion. In 1991, the OGB was home to the popular Saudi Arabia display, followed in 1992 by a collection of "Backyard Monster Bugs." In 1993 the building was the site of the CNE Casino, which continued to occupy the tired old building up until last year. The CNE Casino has again been relocated, this time to the Better Living Centre (gambling = better living?).

Having been home to dice and playing cards, unique handicrafts, and a wide assortment of automobiles, the Ontario Government Building is now undergoing a multi-million-dollar reawakening. Many of the building's unique heritage features are being retained and enhanced, and will soon be appreciated by a whole new generation. For further details on visits to and bookings of what is now known as the Liberty Grand Entertainment Complex, call 416-504-9435 or visit www.libertygroup.com.

August 26, 2001

Moving Toronto

It was eighty years ago yesterday that Robert Ferguson, of 285 Brunswick Avenue, boarded a westbound King streetcar at the King and Yonge corner, deposited his fare, and in doing so, entered the history books as the TTC's first paying customer.

To be historically accurate, the TTC (originally known as the Toronto Transportation Commission) had actually come into existence a little more than a year earlier (June 4, 1920) when the Province of Ontario gave official assent to an Act Respecting the City of Toronto, specifically, Chapter 144, 10-11 George V. The new Commission's mandate was broadly defined and dealt with such matters as the "construction, control, maintenance, operation and management of new lines of street railways in addition to or in extension of existing lines" in the City of Toronto.

Up until the time Mr. Ferguson deposited his fifteen-cent fare at 12:01 a.m. on September 1, 1921, (his was a special "night" fare, the regular daytime fare being seven cents, a full two cents more than that charged by the former operator, but that's another story) Toronto's transportation needs had been served by a succession of private operators. To be sure, the city did attempt to run the system on its own in 1891, but after a trial period of less than four months it decided to return control to a private entrepreneur by the name of William Mackenzie.

A very rare view of an open electric streetcar similar to #327, one of the parade participants. This one, #329, is seen at some unidentified point on the Arthur route, a fact that means the photo was taken sometime between 1902 (the year the route began) and 1909 (the year the route was merged with Dundas).

With little regard for the customer (but full regard for the financial bottom line) Mackenzie's Toronto Railway Company (TRC) continued to have its way for nearly thirty years. It had a monopoly on the lucrative short-haul routes within the most populated parts of the city. Other citizens residing in the outlying areas had to rely on the city-owned, but fragmented, Toronto Civic Railways (TCR) or do without. Eventually, public displeasure with the TRC's refusal to add new routes to serve fast-growing areas outside the city core or to purchase additional modern equipment to replace outdated and unsafe vehicles forced the city fathers to re-think the existing situation.

To bring the matter to a head, civic authorities placed the question as to whether the city should again assume ownership of the transportation system on the 1920 civic election ballot. The reply was overwhelmingly in the affirmative. Once the enabling legislation was in place, the TTC began to implement a well-thought-out program that would see, amongst other things, the eventual consolidation of the TRC's routes and those of its subsidiaries, plus those of the Civic Railways, into one integrated system operating on more customer-friendly timetables and under one city-wide fare schedule.

In addition, new streetcars were purchased, older equipment upgraded, brand new routes laid out, and modern repair facilities con-

On the Danforth in the early 1950s, a Peter Witt and a PCC (similar to those in Thursday's parade celebrating the TTC's eightieth birthday) pass in front of Stoney's Car Market, a popular used car lot not far from the Jones Avenue intersection.

structed. To serve some of the less populated and heretofore neglected areas of the city, gasoline-powered buses were purchased, the first eight of which were of the double-decker, solid tire variety, the most modern then available. These vehicles were used as feeders to the TTC's original streetcar lines just as today's fleet of nearly fifteen hundred buses feed the city's busy subway routes.

Over the years the TTC attempted to stay ahead of the game. It built the nation's first subway (the 4.6-mile Yonge line) in 1954 adding extra mileage in 1963 and 1978 with the University and Spadina extensions. More miles were added again in 1973 and 1974 with the opening of the Yonge extensions to York Mills and then to Finch. In 1966, the first part of the Bloor-Danforth line opened, with additions in 1968 and 1980. The billion-dollar Sheppard subway is scheduled to go into service in 2002.

State-of-the-art streetcars have also been an integral part of the TTC fleet with the modern (for the day) Peter Witt model entering service just one month after the TTC came into being. Next came a succession of light-rail vehicles (modern-day terminology for the familiar and friendly word *streetcar*): the PCC Streamliner in 1938 (followed by numerous upgrades), the CLRV in 1979, and its larger brother the ALRV nine years later. Scarborough RT vehicles entered service in

1985. Over the years new, more efficient subway trains have been designed and purchased, as have new diesel and natural gas buses, with portions of the fleet supplemented by rebuilt versions of some of the older diesel-powered vehicles.

Once in the forefront of transit excellence worldwide, the TTC now seems to be caught in a game of catch-up. It would appear that both the federal and provincial governments aren't overly interested in the future of our transit provider. As a result, a scary scenario is unfolding. Without the financial involvement of those two levels of government to assist with the acquisition of replacement vehicles and to ensure the existing system remains in a good state of repair, it looks as if we're all going to be in for a rough ride.

To help celebrate the TTC's eightieth anniversary, a special party is being planned for this coming September 6. Festivities, complete with a huge cake from the folks at the Sheraton Centre, will begin at Nathan Phillips Square at 10:00 A.M. The highlight of the day will be a parade of vintage streetcars along the tracks of several downtown streets (Queen, Spadina, College, Bay, Dundas, and Church back to City Hall). Honoured participants in the parade will be car #327 (a replica of a 1893 open electric streetcar that was built for the city's centennial in 1934 and which is provided courtesy the folks at the Halton County Radial Railway museum), ancient #2766 (which was built in 1923 and is the TTC's last Peter Witt out of a fleet of 575 similar vehicles), PCCs #4500 and #4549 (the last of 745 such cars), a CLRV, and a modern ALRV that will be followed by a bevy of buses.

September 2, 2001

Dying for Recognition

One of the familiar sights to be seen on the highways and byways, towns, villages, and cities throughout our province are the large blue and gold historic plaques erected by the Ontario Heritage Foundation, now numbering more than eleven hundred. The idea of using highly visible and well-written plaques to stimulate the public's interest in the people, places, and events that have made Ontario such a great place to live (or visit) was pioneered back in the 1950s by what was then known as the Archeological and Historic Sites Board of Ontario.

In 1974, that organization became part of the Ontario Heritage Foundation, under whose mandate the plaque recognition program continues — though now with a much wider scope. Originally, the plaques concentrated on the founding of communities or dealt with matters related to Ontario's political or economic heritage. Today, however the subject material for OHF plaques is as varied as is the province's past. There are plaques commemorating First Nations villages, War of 1812 battle sites, unusual land formations (the terraces of Terrace Bay, for instance, which were formed more than twenty thousand years ago), the site of the first Icelandic settlement in Ontario (this plaque is recorded in three languages), the birthplace of the Ontarian who "invented" basketball (James Naismith of Almonte), as well as the birthplace of the first person to be described as a "movie star" (Toronto's own Gladys Marie Smith, *aka* Mary Pickford). There's

116

even an OHF plaque commemorating the life and times of an animal, one that for many years was known and loved throughout the world. Jumbo the elephant was killed by a train in St. Thomas, Ontario, on September 15, 1885.

Ideas for subject material for OHF commemorative plaques are solicited from the public and, where appropriate, the funds required to research, manufacture, and install the plaques are sought from a variety of sources, including sponsors and donors.

The list of OHF commemorative plaques will be increased once again later this week when Toronto's magnificent Mount Pleasant Cemetery is recognized in this, its 125th year. Officially dedicated on November 4, 1876, Mount Pleasant was established by a group of public-spirited individuals as a non-denominational burial ground. It was to be the eventual successor to their second cemetery, the Necropolis, which was located closer to town on the west bank of the Don River just north of Gerrard. (The trustee's first burial ground was at the northwest corner of today's busy Yonge and Bloor intersection.)

Though well outside the built-up area of the city when established in the 1850s, the Necropolis was now being seriously encroached upon. From a functional viewpoint, the remoteness of the two hundred acres of

It took years to convince Mount Pleasant Cemetery officials that a road should be cut through their property to make north-south travel easier. The thoroughfare, now known as Mt. Pleasant Road and named after the cemetery, was eventually opened, but whether travel was any easier was a moot point for this *circa* 1920 driver.

rolling farm land that would become the new Mount Pleasant was one of the new cemetery's most important features. But it wouldn't be just another burial ground. Its creator, Henry Englehardt, would design it in the style of Mount Auburn Cemetery in Cambridge, Massachusetts. The so-called "landscape cemetery" was an effort to make urban burial grounds resting places not just for the deceased, but for the living as well. With its vast array of trees, shrubs, and bushes, bird life and wildlife, Mount Pleasant is as much a park as it is a cemetery. And as for history, someone once said a cemetery is like a history book with the markers its pages. Mount Pleasant is full of history. It's the final resting place for one Canadian prime minister, eight lieutenant-governors, five premiers, and at least eleven of the city's mayors. Then there's the *Empress of Ireland* and *Noronic* markers, the five city firemen lost in the McIntosh feed factory fire (the only fatalities of the 1904 fire that nearly burned down Toronto), the first Canadian-born female doctor, a survivor of the *Titanic* sinking (who, at times, must have wished he hadn't), and the coach of the last Maple Leaf hockey team to win the Stanley Cup. The list goes on. For more stories see my book *Mount Pleasant Cemetery: An Illustrated Guide* (Dundurn Press, ISBN 1-55002-322-5), available at many bookstores as well as at the cemetery's main office.

September 9, 2001

City's First Superhighway

In an effort to keep up with the ever-increasing number of vehicles trying to get from point A to point B, provincial and local governments continue to spend billions of dollars constructing new roads and improving old ones. Even private enterprise has joined the fray, with the GTA seeing something that earlier governments had declared would never happen, the implementation of toll roads.

That's not to say that this type of thoroughfare had never been seen on our province. In fact, most of the major streets leading to and from Toronto were operated in the early years as toll roads. The reasoning was simple. Back in the early nineteenth century, funds to look after road upkeep were scarce. Officials believed that the prime users of these roads, livestock dealers and farmers off to market to sell their goods, should be forced to pay for the road's maintenance. To make sure this was done, toll booths were erected at strategic locations along the way and fees collected. In fact, for a time a toll gate near the present Yonge and Bloor intersection resulted in the latter thoroughfare being given the name of Tollgate Road.

Eventually, the public forced governments to abandon the use of toll roads throughout the province. Money for building and maintenance of roads came from taxes.

The last toll gates in the Toronto area were closed down effective December 31, 1896. Interestingly, one of the conditions imposed by

119

the York County council before agreeing to end all local tolls was the requirement that the City of Toronto waive all fees charged county residents for space at the busy St. Lawrence Market.

And while the use of toll roads was to disappear for many years (or "forever" as Ontario Premier Leslie Frost kept insisting during his 1949–1961 term of office), the concept was resurrected in June 1997 with the opening of the first stretch of Highway 407, or as they now promote it, 407 ETR, ETR standing for Express Toll Road.

As new and exciting as the promoters of the new 407 ETR would have us believe it is, this highway probably drew no more accolades (or criticisms), relatively speaking that is, than did the opening of Toronto's first "limited access highway" nearly a half-century earlier.

Now before you think that unique roadway was the Gardiner Expressway or perhaps the Don Valley Parkway, it was neither. It was, in fact, what was initially referred to as the Clifton Road Extension. Today we know that special thoroughfare as the Mt. Pleasant Road Extension. And special it was.

When this new thoroughfare was first envisioned in the mid-1920s, Toronto's streets hadn't progressed much past the kind laid out

Jarvis Street at the turn of the century just north of Carlton. The auto age has yet to make much of an impact.

in the city's horse and buggy days. In fact, one of the few advances made in the intervening years was the rounding of corners at major street crossings to permit easier right turns for the cars and trucks found in increasing numbers around town. In addition, a few downtown streets had been paved. But the major drawback to moving more traffic had not been addressed. In fact, the width of newly constructed streets, as well as the established ones, remained at one chain (sixty-six feet) for main streets and half a chain (thirty-three feet) for side streets, identical to the widths adopted by the pioneer surveyors in Governor Simcoe's time. (Spadina Avenue was definitely different. It was cut through the wilderness 2 chains (132 feet) wide. University Avenue, on the other hand, is actually made up of two separate streets, giving it the look of one wide street.)

The new Mt. Pleasant Road Extension would be different. It would be four lanes in width with limited cross street access. Originally, the new street would start (or end) as a continuation of little Clifton Road,

The Mt. Pleasant Road Extension under construction, September 1948. Visible at the top are the CPR main line bridge over the new road, Whitney Public School on the hill, and the curve in the new highway as it approaches St. Clair Avenue.

a neighbourhood street just west of the present Mt. Pleasant Road/St. Clair Avenue intersection. The routing was reworked numerous times so that by the time what was now referred to as the Mt. Pleasant Road Extension was officially opened on May 17, 1950, by Mayor Hiram McCallum it joined Mt. Pleasant Road (at its intersection with St. Clair Avenue) with Jarvis Street at a point south of Bloor Street.

As special as this thoroughfare was, it had its critics. It had too many curves and bends, too many cross streets, too many underpasses, and the hump near Roxborough Road resulted in many drivers losing control of their automobiles if they hit it too fast. In an attempt to slow traffic, police reminded drivers that speed limits would be strictly enforced. Fines were five dollars, plus a dollar for each mile over the limit!

Oh, there was one other criticism. The original estimate for the six-mile thoroughfare was a little over a million dollars. When it was completed three years later that figure had soared to $4.5 million.

September 16, 2001

Junction Name Survives
Many Amalgamations

Many people may think that traffic congestion is a new phenomenon on our city streets. Obviously, as this photograph proves, such is not the case. This view, taken sometime in the early 1920s, looks north on Weston Road from a point a few hundred yards north of St. Clair Avenue West.

Traffic, in the form of horse-drawn farm wagons and newfangled automobiles and trucks, slowly make its collective way towards various markets in the Junction area of Toronto. And looking closely, in the middle of it all a lonely streetcar slowly wends its way northward from its southern terminus in the Junction.

Interestingly, although the term "Junction" was officially abandoned in 1909, it is still very much in use by area residents describing what had first been the village, then the town, of West Toronto Junction. The "Junction" part of the name arose from the fact that this community had grown up around the junction of the pioneer Toronto, Grey and Bruce and Credit Valley railways.

Over the years the community's title was altered with the word *West* dropped. Actually, local officials wanted the word *Junction* removed as it made the community sound like some wide spot in the road. However, the community's main employer, the CPR, demanded the term Junction be retained, as that's what the place was. (And you just knew who was going to win that battle.) So Town of Toronto

Weston Road looking north from north of St. Clair Avenue West in the early 1920s.

Same view, 2001. A few of the buildings in the background of the earlier photo still survive, as does the former powerhouse seen to the right of both views.

Junction it became, with another alteration coming in 1908 when the community was elevated to city status and another new name, City of West Toronto, adopted.

By 1909, even that name vanished when West Toronto became part of the City of Toronto. However, to honour the community's past, many continue to refer to the area as "the Junction." (For more on the history of West Toronto Junction, in all its forms, log onto www.junctionhistory.ca.)

As for the streetcar somewhat buried in the crowd of private vehicles, it was part of the fleet operated by the Toronto Suburban Railway, a company that, in early 1894, brought several small private streetcar lines on the western outskirts of Toronto under one management.

In the same year the Toronto Suburban was incorporated, it constructed an extension of one of the its established lines from the busy Keele and Dundas intersection via Keele Street and Weston Road to the town of Weston some four miles to the north. In 1914, this route was extended another eight miles out into the countryside to the rural community of Woodbridge.

In late 1923, the southerly portion of the Weston-Woodbridge line (Dundas Street to Northland Avenue) was taken over by the recently

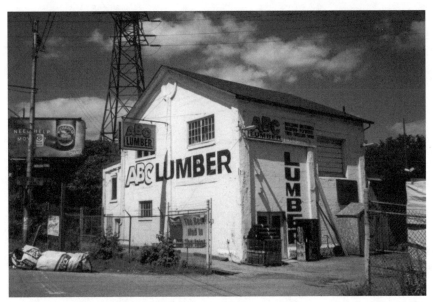

Former Toronto Suburban Railway Co.'s powerhouse turned lumber company sales office, 2001.

established Toronto Transportation Commission. The stretch from Northland to Woodbridge was subsequently divided into three segments that were operated under three distinct owners, the Township of York, the Town of Weston and the Canadian National Railway.

While the Woodbridge connection only lasted until the spring of 1926, the other sections continued on under the supervision of the TTC. Streetcar service from the Junction to Weston ended on September 13, 1948, when buses were substituted.

Back to the subject of traffic congestion for a moment. When one considers the variety of rights-of-way laid out (and planned) for Toronto and its environs (electric cars actually ran to Georgetown, Guelph, Woodbridge, Sutton, Newmarket, and Aurora and were planned for Hamilton, Cobourg, and Peterborough) one has to wonder just how much better commuters would be served today had some of these lines been upgraded rather than simply abandoned.

September 23, 2001

Taking Stock of the Junction

In last week's column I featured an old photo that looked north on Weston Road from a point several hundred yards north of the St. Clair intersection. This week we return to the same area of our city with a pair of photos that again show that part of Weston Road, though this time we look south towards its intersection with Keele Street just north of St. Clair Avenue.

As a point of reference, the buildings just visible along the top of the older photo were on the north side of St. Clair just west of the Keele Street corner. They were the meat processing plants of Swifts and Canada Packers (earlier Harris), companies that because of smells and truck traffic were not always welcome features of the Junction community.

By the way, those who haven't visited this part of town for a while are in for a real surprise. What had been the largest daily livestock market on the continent (covering 250 acres with nearly 10,000 employees) closed for good in early 1994. Soon, those hulking processing plants and the nearby Ontario Stockyard were no more. And today, the area is home to several "big box" retail stores as well as whole new residential community.

In the foreground of the older view, which was taken in the fall of 1925, we see dozens of employees of the four-year-old Toronto Transportation Commission laying new streetcar track that replaced temporary rails in use prior to the realignment of Weston Road.

127

Looking south on Weston Road from McCormack Street, 1925.

Same view, Gunns Road in the background to the right, 2001. The radial railway bridge was demolished several years ago.

Also of interest in the photo is the newly constructed bridge over Weston Road that was used by the electric radial cars (the term *radial* was used to describe this and other similar routes that radiated out from Toronto) of the Toronto Suburban Railway to access its Toronto terminal near the northeast corner of Keele. The western terminal of this high-speed commuter and freight line was in Guelph, Ontario, nearly fifty miles distant. The Suburban served such small communities along the way as Islington, Dixie, Streetsville, Georgetown, and Acton. Radial cars made their last runs to Guelph in 1931. The Halton County Radial Railway museum now operates a fleet of ancient street-cars along part of the company's right-of-way. That bridge was removed only recently.

Another interesting feature of the 1925 photo is the presence of a horse-drawn Eaton's wagon in the foreground. The driver is missing, probably making a delivery nearby.

September 30, 2001

The Evolution of a Corner

Originally, what we now know as Eglinton Avenue was nothing more than a line on a surveyor's map, a line that simply delineated the boundary between Concessions 3 and 4 (north of the Bay) in the Township of York. Further south, similar lines delineated

In this photo, Coon's feed store stands on the northwest corner of Yonge and Eglinton. In 1922, following the TTC's decision to extended its Yonge streetcar line north to a new loop at Glen Echo (City Limits) the little building was moved back from the intersection to permit the widening of the street.

A F.W. Woolworth five-and-dime store and Tamblyn drugstore are the main tenants of the next building to straddle the corner, circa 1966.

Today, stores, restaurants, and offices occupy the busy Yonge and Eglinton corner.

boundaries between Concessions 1 and 2 and Concessions 2 and 3. Those lines have evolved into today's Bloor Street and St. Clair Avenue, respectively.

While communities were quick to develop around the Bloor and Yonge intersection (Yorkville, a village then a town) and the Yonge and St. Clair intersection (Deer Park), the corner of Yonge and Eglinton took longer to develop. In fact, the first permanent structure on the northwest corner, a feed store owned by George Coon (who lived upstairs), didn't appear until the first decade of the twentieth century. Several decades later feed gave way to food when the old building became the popular Eglinton Restaurant.

The old two-storey brick building was pulled down in the late 1940s and a modern office building, with Woolworth, Tamblyn, and Laura Secord stores on the main floor, was erected on the site.

In October 1975, it all changed again when the first version of the new Yonge Eglinton Centre opened. Major renovations and additions in 1997 transformed the corner once again. Is the evolution of this corner complete? Probably not.

October 7, 2001

A "Horrid" City Hall

It's interesting how we get so used to things. There was a time when we were fascinated watching the CN Tower begin its climb ever higher. And when Olga the Sikorsky helicopter arrived in town to put the final pieces in place, just about every pair of eyes downtown was focused skyward.

Then there was the time thousands stood hypnotized as SkyDome's massive roof went through its gyrations as it opened or closed. Sometimes, drivers up on the Gardiner even slowed or stopped right on the Expressway to get a better look.

Even "New" City Hall (though at thirty-six years of age it's hardly new) has become so much a part of our city that very few Torontonians pay it much attention anymore. That in spite of the fact that when its design was officially announced in late September 1958 its unique appearance had tongues wagging not just here in Toronto, but all across the country as well.

The selection of the design provided by forty-two-year-old Finnish architect Viljo Revell (initially spelled Rewell in the newspapers) came as a result of a worldwide competition. However, this wasn't the first time an attempt was made to get a new municipal office for our city. In fact, it wasn't long after what we now refer to as "Old" City Hall opened in the fall of 1899 that the building was described as being inadequate for the needs of the fast growing city.

The original architect's model (on the left of this photo) had the taller tower of Toronto's new City Hall on the west side. For whatever reason, the plan was subsequently revised, resulting in the taller tower being on the right. In addition, a proposed high-class restaurant that was to be located on the top floor of the East Tower never materialized.

As inadequate as it may have been, the old building continued to serve as Toronto's city hall for decades. Then, as part of the election ballot for the year 1956, voters were asked if they favoured the "erecting and equipping of a new City Hall on the Civic Square at a new capital expenditure of $13.5 million." Interestingly, the Civic Square referred to had already been acquired as a result of a similar municipal election ballot held eight years earlier. No matter, the electorate turned the idea down flat, with 32,640 against and only 28,497 approving the idea. The city hall we already had would just have to do. Undaunted, politicians had the question of a new city hall placed on the following year's ballot, and this time the proposal was approved 31,814 to 26,811. Close, but the go-ahead had finally been given.

With the necessary approval now in place, each of the three local architectural firms was asked to come up with their concept for a new city hall. They were then asked to select which of the three concepts they felt would best suit the city's needs. Not surprisingly, this was an unworkable idea. It was then that Mayor Nathan Phillips came up with the idea of a competition open not only to Canadian architects, but to architects from all over the world. For obvious reasons his idea wasn't all that popular at home. Nevertheless, the mayor ultimately got his way, and it wasn't long before dozens and dozens of submissions began arriving. As it turned out, the judges had to choose from 520 proposals submitted by architects who represented 42 different countries.

From the 520 submissions eight finalists were selected, five from the United States and one each from Canada, Denmark, and Finland. From that group, the design submitted by Viljo Revell from Finland was chosen as the winner, a decision that was announced on September 26, 1958.

Revell teamed up with Toronto architect John Parkin, and work on the new structure finally began in late 1961. A little less than four years later (September 13, 1965, to be precise) Toronto's new City Hall was officially opened by Governor General George Vanier. However, not everyone appreciated the design. Some called it "horrid, not of this world," others thought it was just "odd," while the celebrated American architect Frank Lloyd Wright (who did not enter the competition) called it "a piece of architectural sterility."

October 14, 2001

An impossible view today as the Sheraton Centre now sits on the site of a short-lived park.

The Legacy Continues

When Lady Eaton and her son John David officially opened the new Eaton's College Street store on October 30, 1930, there was every indication that this massive building would eventually replace both the "ancient" store at the northwest corner of Yonge and Queen streets (that had grown like crazy over the past four decades) as well as the nearby factories where a variety of Eaton products were made. What they were opening was just the first phase of what many believed would ultimately be a thirty-six-storey building, complete with a skyscraping art deco–style tower.

The idea of moving away from the Yonge and Queen corner had its inception twenty years earlier when company president (and son of founder Timothy Eaton) John Craig Eaton began purchasing property in and around the Yonge-College-Carlton corners. The term *corners* is used because at that time College and Carlton streets abutted Yonge Street at two separate locations, forming two separate and distinct corners (see photo).

Eaton chose this area because it was felt by many businessmen of the day, including him, that this corner would soon become the fast-growing city's new downtown. As it turned out, development moved quicker than anyone thought, with the Yonge-Bloor corner to the north becoming Toronto's new "heart" instead.

With the outbreak of the Great War in 1914, plans for the relocation

Yonge Street looking south at College Street with the disconnected Carlton Street corner at left, *circa* 1911.

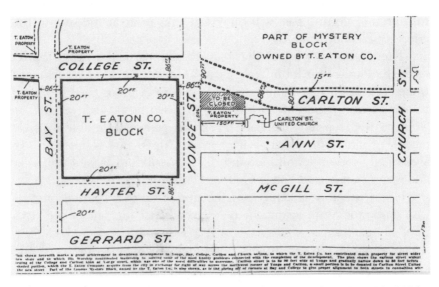

Map of this intersection from the *Evening Telegram*, October 18, 1930.

of the Eaton interests to the new site were put on hold. Then, in 1922, John Craig Eaton (now Sir John in honour of his efforts, financial and philanthropic, during the war) passed away, the victim of pneumonia. It was his wife, the former Flora McCrae, who kept the idea of a fine new Eaton structure uptown alive. With the assistance of Robert Young Eaton, Sir John's cousin, who took over company operations following Sir John's untimely death, work on the new Eaton's College Street store began.

While the store as first envisioned (670 feet in height with five million square feet of retail space) never did materialize, Eaton's College Street was, and remains, a remarkable structure and a true Toronto landmark.

Eaton's presence on the Yonge and College corner ended on February 5, 1977, when all downtown store operations were moved to north end of the new Eaton Centre. The old building was then remodeled, reopening in 1979 as College Park, a collection of retail shops, offices, and provincial law courts.

Today, work is underway to once again revamp the former Eaton's College Street store. This time it appears as if the legendary Eaton Auditorium, which opened on the seventh floor on March 26, 1931, (where almost all of Glenn Gould's recording endeavours were carried out before the auditorium's closure in 1976) will be part of the new facility, as will the Round Room restaurant. These two landmark features from Toronto's past will survive thanks in great measure to the efforts of Eleanor Koldofsky.

There is another legacy that motorists, in particular, enjoy thanks to the building of Sir John Craig Eaton's College Street store. As mentioned earlier in the column, Sir John acquired various parcels of land in and around the future site of his proposed new headquarters. As work on the store commenced, the Eaton people were able to trade parcels of land with other nearby owners, deals that resulted in the abnormally wide sidewalks around the new building as well as a safer and easier to navigate Yonge-College-Carlton intersection.

It was the announcement of the new store that spurred officials into proposing, once again, the redesign of what was one of the city's most dangerous intersections. Up until then College and Carlton streets were two separate streets, both commencing at Yonge, with the Carlton Street corner being over one hundred feet south of where College met Yonge. This resulted in the Carlton route streetcars, which operated on both College and Carlton streets, having to make a dangerous double turn as they crossed the city's main street, Yonge.

East- and westbound vehicular traffic also had to make this awkward and frequently dangerous manoeuvre.

Mayoralty candidate Bert Wemp made elimination of this serious traffic situation one of his election platforms. It no doubt helped him win the 1930 election, defeating incumbent Sam McBride, something the feisty McBride never forgot. Eaton's concurred, and together the city and the T.Eaton Company proceeded with the necessary arrangements.

The plans for the realignment of College and Carlton streets can be seen on the accompanying map, which was featured in the October 18, 1930, *Evening Telegram* newspaper. Note also that the Eaton's company owned the land on which Maple Leaf Gardens would be built. Almost exactly one year after these plans appeared the first hockey game was held in the new Gardens. Incidentally, Ann Street was renamed Granby, and only that part of Hayter Street west of Bay remains.

The new Yonge-College-Carlton intersection opened for streetcar traffic in early June 1931.

October 21, 2001

Dig Solves Mystery

Okay, I admit it. I have a rather strange obsession. Well, not an obsession really. Perhaps fascination is a better word. I'm fascinated by how and why streets here in our city got their respective names.

And while in most cases there's an obvious reason for giving a street a particular name (Front Street = at the front of the townsite, Bay Street = running to and from the bay, etc.), some names just don't make any sense at all. For instance, the term Parliament Street, when applied to a thoroughfare several miles east of the Legislative Building of Ontario (or more simply, the Parliament Buildings), in the minds of many just doesn't compute.

But the recent discovery of parts of our province's first Parliament Buildings under yards of asphalt has made the reason for the street's name obvious. That's because those buildings were located south of Front Street and west of, wait for it, Parliament Street.

To truly understand the significance of this find we have to go back to the year 1791 and the appointment of John Graves Simcoe as the first lieutenant-governor of the recently created Province of Upper Canada (renamed Ontario in 1867). To administer to the needs of his new responsibility it became necessary for Simcoe to establish a place where his governing officials could meet. That honour initially went Newark (now Niagara-on-the-Lake). This turned out to be not the best of locations, considering its proximity to the

140

Sketches of the province's first Parliament Buildings are few and far between. The buildings are seen in this small sketch that appeared in Eric Arthur's 1979 book, *Front Street to Queen's Park*.

The York Hotel (on the site of the Toronto Sun building), where parliament was held after Americans burned the buildings in the top sketch.

border with the United States, which then was not the friendly country it is today.

In 1794 Simcoe agreed to establish a "temporary" provincial capital at York (now Toronto) with every intention of eventually having a permanent version located at a place we now know as London, Ontario. It was while York served as this temporary seat of government that the recently uncovered parliament buildings were erected.

Obviously Simcoe didn't move his capital far enough from the U.S. border, since these rudimentary structures were burned during an attack on our community by American army and naval forces in April 1813, just one of many bitter battles during what has become known as the War of 1812.

On the other hand, views of the present Parliament Buildings at the top of University Avenue abound. This is a *circa* 1900 postcard view showing the 1893 structure before a devastating fire destroyed much of the west wing. The restoration added an extra floor and rendered the front facade of the building no longer symmetrical.

Whether that fire was accidental or intentional has yet to be determined. Nevertheless, the loss of the small brick structures resulted in the Parliament of Upper Canada (by now a permanent feature of York, Simcoe's plans for the London site having vanished with the lieutenant-governor's departure from the province in 1796) being forced to meet in a variety of buildings around town, including a short stint in the York Hotel that stood on the site of the present Toronto Sun building.

When it came time to build a new home for parliament, and with money in short supply, officials decided to simply recycle the original government buildings, enlarging them somewhat by constructing a new section that would join the two outer buildings. This modified structure was ready in time for parliament to meet therein in December 1820.

Once again, however, fire was to visit the site. This time sparks from an overheated chimney resulted in the building's total destruction on the evening of December 30, 1824. Again parliament was forced to meet in various locations around town, but never again on the site of the original buildings.

That site was eventually cleared, and over the succeeding years a variety of structures went up on the Front and Parliament site, including a jail and the sprawling Consumers' Gas Station "A" complex of buildings, one component of which still stands on the south side of Front opposite John Hood's mural of the history of Toronto on the rear of the Toronto Sun building. In recent years the old Parliament Building site has been home to automotive-related businesses including car and truck repair shops and car washes.

This brings us up the present, or at least up to the fall of last year when Heritage Toronto, prompted by the group Citizens of the Old Town and financially supported by the city and the present property owners, Budget Car Rentals and Auto World Imports, contracted with Archeological Services, Inc. to examine the site in-depth, both literally and figuratively. And what that examination disclosed was that remnants of our province's first Parliament Buildings still exist under tons of asphalt in the heart of old York.

The history of this fascinating period in our province's history, as well as how the archeological dig was conducted and what artifacts were actually found, is presented in a richly illustrated new book from eastendbooks, *Government on Fire*, by Frank Dieterman and Ronald Williamson (ISBN 1-896973-26-4).

October 28, 2001

Deer Roamed Here

This great and marvellous city of ours is actually made up of dozens of smaller communities that over the past 118 years have joined together to create what we now refer to as the "new" City of Toronto. The first to join the original city was Yorkville on the city's northern edge. This annexation occurred in 1883 and obviously increased both the size of Toronto as well as its population. Over the next few years other communities joined, the largest of them being Seaton Village (near the present Bloor and Bathurst intersection), the City of West Toronto (in and around Keele and Dundas), Midway (in the city's east end), and the Town of North Toronto. In fact, between 1883 and 1914 a total of thirty-two separate additions were made. These ranged in size from a mere three acres along Summerhill Avenue to the aforementioned four-square-mile parcel known as the Town of North Toronto. When the dust had finally settled these annexations had increased the area of the city from its original 8.7 square miles to more than 30, in a period of just three decades.

While each of the communities absorbed by the city had its own unique history, one in particular emphasizes just how much Toronto has been transformed.

Deer Park was described as sitting astride Yonge Street with its north and south boundaries at Mount Pleasant Cemetery and the CPR tracks respectively; a pair of ravines bracketed it, the Nordheimer to the west and the Rosedale (also known as the Vale of Avoca) to the east.

144

St. Clair Avenue looking west from Yonge Street *circa* 1910.

The same view today.

The area obtained its name from the forty-acre estate at the north-west corner of today's busy Yonge/St. Clair intersection owned by one Agnes Heath, a Scottish lady whose husband had been killed in 1818 during the Deccan War in India. Agnes and her young family eventually immigrated to Upper Canada, purchasing land at the corner of Yonge Street and something called the Third Concession. Here she built a house on an estate Agnes called Deer Park because of the large herd of deer that would frequently appear in the backyard of the house looking for food.

As the years passed, portions of the estate were sold off to developers, one of whom was Weymouth Schreiber. Schreiber's wife was the former Harriet De Lisle, whose surname was subsequently given to one of the streets laid out through the Heath estate. Another street, Lawton Boulevard, took its name from Lawton Park, a six-acre piece of land carved from the Heath estate by another early settler in this part of York Township, Col. Arthur Cathew.

Interestingly, Lawton Boulevard was to be the original right-of-way of Yonge Street. However, when the pioneer surveyors realized there'd be a problem connecting the lower portion of Yonge with the upper portion that had been laid out well to the east, an eastward deflection of the street was quickly made. This bend can be seen where Lawton Boulevard now enters Yonge Street.

Oh, and in case you haven't already figured it out, the Third Concession now goes by the name St. Clair Avenue. How it got that name is a case of pure speculation. Some believe it was named in honour of Augustine St. Clair (also spelled Clare), a character in Harriet Beecher Stowe's book *Uncle Tom's Cabin*, an extremely popular novel during the time the Deer Park area was being settled.

For more information on this area of Toronto, pick up a copy of Joan Kinsella's 1996 booklet "Historical Walking Tour of Deer Park," published by and available from the Toronto Public Library.

November 4, 2001

Hero's Final Journey

The eleventh hour of the eleventh day of the eleventh month.
Lest We Forget.

In May 2000, Canada brought its "unknown soldier" home and gave him a place of prominence and dignity in the nation's capital city. That soldier's identity was closely guarded, and all we really know about him is that he was one of the 1,603 who made the supreme sacrifice on the battlefields of Vimy Ridge, the site of the First World War conflict in which Canadian troops fought as a combined force for the first time.

Many will recall the solemn events associated with the transferring of remains from a quiet cemetery near Souchez, France, to the Tomb of the Unknown Soldier at the National War Memorial on Parliament Hill in Ottawa. Here, this Canadian hero represents the more than twenty-eight thousand other Canadian heroes who have fought in too many wars and have no known grave. His arrival home was in great measure a result of the efforts of the Royal Canadian Legion. And while it had taken more than eighty years for Canada to honour its "unknown soldier" (Britain, the United States, and France had each done their duty many years earlier), that unfortunate situation wasn't for a lack of trying by a young suburban Toronto church minister.

Robert Currie Creelman had ministered to the needs of members of the Weston Presbyterian Church on Cross Street for several years. Then,

The Reverend Robert Currie Creelman, padre of the First Hussars, RCAC.

with the outbreak of the Second World War, his responsibilities changed when he became Major the Rev. R.C. Creelman, Padre of the First Hussars, Royal Canadian Armoured Corp of London, Ontario.

A few weeks before D-Day, Creelman found himself within the solemn greatness of London, England's Westminster Abbey, where, for some unexplained reason, he was drawn to its Warrior's Tomb. *Why doesn't something similar exist back home?* he pondered.

Several weeks later the Allies crossed the Channel and advanced on German forces. The Reverend Major Creelman stayed with his men, looking after their needs as best he could. In mid-August 1944, the Canadians advanced on first Caen, then Bretteville, and finally on to Falaise. It was here that one of the bloodiest battles of the war was fought. Soon the once peaceful fields were littered with dead and dying men and dozens of burned-out tanks. Acting suddenly, Creelman entered one of the fire-ravaged Canadian tanks and recovered the remains of one of its occupants. In the padre's mind, these ashes would represent his country's "unknown soldier." Creelman eventually placed the ashes in an urn and carried them with him throughout the rest of the war. Months later, and with victory finally achieved, the Canadians slowly made their way home, Creelman returning on the *Empress Of Scotland* late in 1945. With him were the remains he had taken from the burned-out tank. Once back at his Weston, Ontario, church, he gave the urn a place of reverence on the communion table. He then attempted to have his government prepare a proper national memorial chapel and tomb in which this "unknown soldier" could finally be placed at rest. At first it looked as if the new military hospital under construction on

The Boulton family headstone in Mount Pleasant Cemetery. Incorporated in the marker is a cross made out of stones that marked the grave of Captain Stewart Boulton, who was killed in action at Vimy Ridge on April 4, 1917. The captain's remains were subsequently moved to a French cemetery.

Bayview Avenue north of Toronto would be the repository. Certainly, he thought, the chapel at Sunnybrook would be a fitting place. But it was not to be. In fact, the government decreed that under no circumstance would Creelman's "unknown soldier" be allowed his final rest here in Canada, the country for which he had fought and for which he had given his life. As harsh it may seem, the reason for the government's decision was based on the premise that all men were created equal and that rank and financial status were of no consequence (unlike during the First World War, when families who could afford it could have their soldiers brought home to bury).

In the spring of 1946, Rev. Creelman's "unknown soldier" was taken back to the spot where he was found and buried in a nearby cemetery. The urn was accompanied by Maj. John Foote, the heroic padre of the August 1942 Dieppe raid and a recipient of the Victoria Cross.

November 11, 2001

Magic Movie Memories

As I've mentioned in previous columns, I was an inner-city kid. I spent the first few years of what I hope will be a long life not far from the corner of Bloor and Bathurst streets. My early education was served up at Palmerston Avenue Public School, and I learned the basics of being a good sport under the guidance of Mr. Harris at the local "K" club. In the evenings I listened to *The Adventures of Superman* and *Sergeant Preston of the Yukon* on the family radio and on weekends played Cowboys and Indians (can you still say that?) with my pal Joey DiCresce in the laneway behind our third-floor "hot water flat."

Back then we didn't have any McDonald's or Wendy's, nor did we have shopping centres (they had yet to be invented; the city's first would appear at the Bayview-Eglinton corner years later). In fact, the closest restaurant to our place was Peter's Lunch on the south side of Bloor Street just west of the Bathurst corner, and all the family's shopping was confined to either the Loblaw's store at the Bloor and Bathurst corner ("Remember", my mother would warn, "get hamburger, not the more expensive round steak mince.") or to the Kresge or Woolworth stores on the north side of Bloor, the former east of Bathurst, the latter west. However, more serious shopping demanded a trip downtown to Eaton's main store.

A lengthy trip for me was a voyage on the Bathurst streetcar to the far distant Wychwood branch of the public library way up north near the

One of the Allen family's chain of premier theatres, the Major was at 1780 St. Clair Avenue near the corner of Old Weston Road. This view was taken in 1945.

More than a half-century later the old theatre, features of which are still visible, is home to a bank where Jesus Saves. Just kidding. The building is now a church.

St. Clair Avenue corner. And if I got lost I was instructed to look for a policeman and give him my name and phone number. And while I occasionally forget my name, I'll never forget that number: MElrose 2154.

Now all of this may sound like a pretty boring existence, especially when compared with all the attractions kids have to choose from these days. But there was something we had back then that is sorely missing from the today's itinerary. We had a collection of our very own neighbourhood movie theatres. Not the sterile, fifty or so seat multi-screen kind you find in today's malls. Oh no, ours were cavernous, or at least it seemed so to us kids. And each had a special smell that probably evolved from a mixture of popcorn, Nibs licorice pieces, and a dash of Vernor's ginger ale. We sat in some sort of brushed cloth seat and stared at a screen that usually had a hole or at least a tear in it. And in the background you could hear the whir of the projector and if you watched real close you could tell by the little circle in the upper right corner when the reels of film were ready to be switched over. Some projectionists would be good at the switch, but some left a gaping dead spot as Roy Rogers, Gene Autry, or Whip Wilson chased the bad guys across the screen. And once in a while the bulb would blow, resulting in neither motion nor picture.

I lived in a particularly good part of town with at least four locals to choose from. To the west along Bloor Street was the Metro, to the east the Midtown and the Bloor. The latter is now the site of a restaurant while the former, originally known as the Madison, was eventually renamed the Bloor. And of course there was my favourite, the Alhambra. That was probably because the theatre manager, Pat Tobin, took a liking to me for some reason. He'd invite me over on Sundays to help clean the place, my payment being as much day-old popcorn as I could eat. Today, a Swiss Chalet sits on the site.

Back then, regardless of where you lived, everyone had his or her favourite theatre. And they had such great names: KUM-C, Royal George, Orpheum, Apollo, and the Palace. There were dozens of others, many of which are featured in John Sebert's marvellous new book titled *The "Nabes": Toronto's Wonderful Neighbourhood Theatres* ($25, Mosaic Press). ("Nabes" is defined in the Random House dictionary as slang for neighbourhood theatres.)

November 18, 2001

Booking Christmas

As the gift giving season approaches it's not surprising that once again bookstores all over town have stocked their shelves with a whole bunch of new titles. And that's precisely why I am devoting this week's column to the subject of new books. Not, however, to the books that get big play in the stores, but rather to those Canadian works that never seem to see the light of day. More specifically, let me tell you about a few titles that are devoted to subjects related to our country's fascinating past. To make finding the books a bit easier I've included the book's author, publisher, price, and International Standard Book Number, a code unique to each work that will enable any bookseller to order that specific book. And don't let them tell you they can't. If the big guys give you a hassle try your local corner bookstore. I know they'd love the business.

Canadian aviation expert Larry Milberry has done it again with the latest volume in his series, *Canada's Air Force at War and Peace* (CANAV Books, $85, ISBN 0-921022-13-1). This lavishly illustrated (1,500 black-and-white photos), 520 page, hardcover work looks at the post-war period during which the RCAF downsized then had to scramble to re-equip for the Korean conflict. The Cold War era followed and again the RCAF found itself in a difficult situation. Then came unification of the Forces and more uncertainties during the 1970s. Of special interest is a chapter on the AVRO Arrow, a Canadian creation that was originally proposed

One of the many interesting photos in Larry Milberry's new book is this view of F-86 Sabres over the Toronto waterfront in the 1950s. Note the city's Island Airport and the old Maple Leaf baseball stadium at the foot of Bathurst Street, which was demolished in 1968.

as the twin-engined fighter that would put the RCAF well ahead of any air force operating anywhere the world. Milberry's take on the project is not something that the Arrow enthusiast will find very flattering. Also available are the first two volumes in what will eventually be a quartet devoted to the history of Canada's much respected, much criticized air force. Milberry's new book is available at Aviation World (phone 416-674-5959), from the author (416-698-7559), or from the Toronto Sun News Research Centre (416-947-2258 or 1-877-624-1463).

Another aspect of Canada's role in military matters is told in great detail in *Camp X, the Final Battle* (self-published, ISBN 0-9687062-3-1), a new book by Lynn-Philip Hodgson and Alan Paul Longfield. Camp X was a secret school for spies located on the shores of Lake Ontario, not far from what was still a very rural community known as Whitby. In Hodgson's first book on the subject, *Inside Camp X*, the history of the camp and the lives of its staff and trainees was documented. In this new book the authors look at the chilling scenario of what would have happened had the German invasion of Britain been undertaken and carried on to a successful conclusion. Recently uncovered documents prepared by Winston Churchill reveal that had the unthinkable happened, Camp X and Canada would have played a major role in the ultimate defeat of the enemy.

Flying Under Fire (Fifth House Ltd., $21.95, ISBN 1-894004-79-5) is a compilation of first-hand accounts by RCAF pilots, trainees, and ground crew who recall the danger, excitement, and tragedy encountered while serving their country during the Second World War.

Doing Good by J.T.H. Connor (University of Toronto Press, $60, ISBN 0-8020-4774-2) tells in fascinating detail the story behind the evolution of the Toronto General Hospital from its on-again, off-again origins in a small two-storey structure at the northwest corner of King and John streets to its present prestigious position as one of the world's finest hospitals.

1,000 Questions About Canada (Hounslow, $22.99, ISBN 0-88882-232-4) are asked by Canada's premier trivia buff, John Robert Colombo, in this new book. For instance, are any Canadians buried in Arlington National Cemetery? What is poutine, and who developed it? Have any Canadians been abducted by aliens? Pressing questions to be sure. And there are 997 more.

In author Glen Northcliffe's *The Ride to Modernity, the Bicycle in Canada 1869–1900* (University of Toronto Press, $24.95, ISBN 0-8020-8205-X), the impact of the bicycle on the economic, social, and technological history of our country is examined. Included are dozens of rare old photographs showing cycle-riding Canadians at work and play.

I'll drink to the success of Allen Winn Sneath's new book, *Brewed in Canada, the Untold Story of Canada's 350-year-old Brewing Industry* (Dundurn Press, $24.99, ISBN 1-55002-364-0).

When you hear the term Marks Brothers you probably immediately think of Groucho, Chico, Harpo (and sometimes Zeppo). But note the spelling of that surname. The aforementioned were the American brothers Marx. Here in Canada we had Robert, John, Joseph, Thomas, Alex, Ernest, and McIntyre, often described as the country's most remarkable theatrical family. Their extraordinary story is told in Michael Taylor's *The Canadian Kings of Repertoire* (Natural Heritage, $24.95, ISBN 1-896219-76-4).

November 25, 2001

A Small Mystery

It was on this day exactly eighty-two years ago that one of the greatest mysteries in Toronto's history began to unfold. It all started soon after the city's well-known theatre impresario, fifty-two-year-old Ambrose Small, successfully concluded arrangements to sell his various theatres throughout Southern Ontario to Trans-Canada Theatres Ltd. The deal was for $1.75 million, an enormous amount of money for the time.

One of those theatres was the fashionable Grand Opera House located on the south side of Adelaide Street, just steps west of the Yonge Street corner. (The present Grand Opera Lane marks its east boundary.) The theatre was built by Alexander Manning (Manning Avenue) and opened to the public in 1874. Just five years later it was totally destroyed by fire. However, the Grand was so popular that its new owners rushed its reconstruction, opening to an eager public just fifty-one days after the blaze. It was while the Grand was under the management of the popular O.B. Sheppard (remembered in the nearby Sheppard Street) that Small got his first taste of the theatrical world when he was hired as the assistant manager. Unfortunately, Small could often be an unfriendly cuss, and it was this trait that eventually got him fired. On the day he left the Grand, Small warned Sheppard that he would return one day. That prophecy was to come true.

As the years passed, Small extended his theatre holdings many times over, using methods both fair and not so fair. But his interests in show

$50,000 REWARD

Missing from his home in this city since December 2nd, 1919

Ambrose J. Small

I am authorized by Mrs. Ambrose J. Small and Capital Trust Corporation to offer a reward of $50,000 for information leading to the discovery of the present whereabouts of the above named man, if alive.

Description: Age 53, 5ft. 6 or 7 ins.; 135 to 140 lbs. Blue eyes, sallow complexion. Brown hair and moustache, streaked with grey. Hair receding on temples. Is very quick in his movements.

Mr. Small, who is well known in theatrical circles in the United States and Canada, was owner of Grand Opera House, Toronto, and was last seen in his office at this theatre on afternoon of December 2nd, 1919.

When last seen he was wearing a dark tweed suit and dark overcoat with velvet collar and a soft felt hat.

The above photo, although taken some time ago is a good likeness, except that for a considerable time previous to his disappearance he had been wearing his moustache clipped short.

I am also authorized to offer in the alternative, a reward of $15,000 for information leading to the discovery of the present whereabouts of the body of the above named man, if dead.

The information must be received before September 1st, 1920, on which date the above offers of rewards will expire.

All previous offers of rewards are withdrawn.

Wire all information to the undersigned.

H. J. GRASETT,
Chief Constable.

POLICE HEADQUARTERS.
TORONTO
June 1st. 1920.

The mysterious Ambrose Small.

Small was the assistant manager and later owner of the Grand Opera House on Adelaide Street West. Some Torontonians thought he was (or should have been) dispatched in the theatre's massive furnace.

business soon waned. Looking for new challenges, Small decided to sell his holdings, a total of six theatres that included the Grand here in Toronto as well as a theatre with the same name in London, Ontario. The mammoth deal closed on December 2, 1919, and when all the papers had been signed, Small was handed a cheque for $1 million with $750,000 to follow. Small took the cheque to his bank, deposited it, and left.

Now here's where the mystery begins. When Ambrose Small walked out of the bank he apparently walked off the face of the earth.

He hasn't been seen since, dead or alive.

Mrs. Small, believing that her husband had simply gone on one of his frequent "benders," hesitated to call in the police. A whole month passed before she sought their help, and when she did, it wasn't long before the story became a major news item in newspapers across the country.

Soon the hunt was on to locate the missing millionaire. An old dump not far from the Small residence at 51 Glen Road was dug up. Nothing. Before long, both the house itself and the furnace of the theatre came under scrutiny. Still nothing. Small, or even small pieces of Small, was nowhere to be found. Finally, in December 1927, eight years after his disappearance, Small was declared legally dead. To this very day, exactly eighty-two years after he walked out of the bank, the disappearance of Ambrose Small has yet to be solved.

December 2, 2001

Our Long and Winding Roads

Attempts to improve Toronto's traffic woes are not new. In my October 21, 2001, column I wrote about how the present Yonge-College-Carlton intersection came about as a result of city officials deciding to rebuild what had been both a complicated and dangerous corner. That project, which was undertaken more than seventy years ago, helped speed up traffic while making a very dangerous intersection safer for pedestrians and motorists alike. Even older was the decision made by the city fathers in the early 1900s to turn our present Dundas Street into a cross-town traffic artery. Historically, the original Dundas Street bears little resemblance to the modern-day thoroughfare that runs from Toronto's boundary with Mississauga to its junction with Kingston Road many miles to the east.

The route as originally laid out by the province's first lieutenant-governor, John Graves Simcoe, was an attempt to connect the naval outpost at York (later Toronto) with a site on the Thames River (in London), which Simcoe anticipated would someday become the location of the provincial capital. To trace the street's original route within our present city boundaries, we would follow Ossington Avenue from its intersection with Queen north, then west along the present Dundas Street. Back then Dundas didn't run east of Ossington and therefore there was no Yonge-Dundas intersection.

159

Looking south on Yonge just south of Dundas, 1949.

Years later, when officials decided to create a new cross-town traffic artery, Dundas was extended easterly by simply joining together a number of smaller east-west streets along the proposed routing. That's why the modern Dundas Street, east of Ossington, is such a disjointed thoroughfare with lots of curves and bends. Absorbed into the Dundas Street we know today were streets such as (from west to east) Arthur, St. Patrick, Agnes, Crookshank, and Wilton. Much of this work was completed by 1918. Years later, a group of even smaller streets through the community lying east of the Don River were joined together, allowing Dundas to connect up with the Kingston Road.

Today, many of the connecting points along Dundas Street remain as bends or curves. They can be found at Bathurst (where old Arthur was diverted to connect with St. Patrick), University (where St. Patrick linked with Agnes), and Yonge (where Agnes connected with Crookshank). Interestingly, part of old Crookshank can be seen in today's Dundas Square. This photo looks south on Yonge Street from Dundas one snowy night in March. The Imperial Theatre opened in 1920 as Pantages, was renamed Imperial, renamed again as the Imperial Six, then beautifully restored under its original name, Pantages. The streetcar in the view is what were known as three-man (one operator and two conductors) Witt trains. Witt was the model type, named after its creator, Cleveland, Ohio, transit official Peter Witt. These cars are actually on the Yonge route. However, with the city's first subway under construction, Yonge Street was frequently torn up. With Yonge south of Dundas torn up streetcars, got around the problem by operating over track on Dundas, Victoria, and Richmond streets.

December 9, 2001

* Pantages is now the Canon Theatre. The Downtown theatre buildings to the left of the view were demolished for the new Dundas Square.

Our Man Filey Is Stumped

Having written this column now for more than a quarter of a century (I was just a baby when I started), it's perhaps only natural that readers occasionally ask if I ever run out of story ideas. Obviously, the answer is no. Why? Because the history of our city, though not long in years, is made up of thousands of stories, both fascinating and entertaining. Thus far, this column has only scratched the surface.

There's another aspect of Toronto's past that just as interesting and just as diverse. That's the city's history as captured in the work of some of the city's pioneering photographers. And not just in the creations by professionals such as Alexander Galbraith, Josiah Bruce, or the experts at Pringle and Booth. There are also those images captured by the amateur photographers of yesteryear. Unfortunately, more often than not we have no idea who actually snapped the picture or even when it was taken. That second problem can often be solved with a little detective work.

Accompanying this column are three old photos that I've recently received from three different readers. I know quite a bit about two of them and virtually nothing about the third. Let's look at this mystery photo first.

This photo shows a local Toronto baseball team on its way to a game. All I really know is that one of the people in the view is George "Lefty" Westlake (his daughter sent me the photo) and the photo was taken sometime between 1913 and 1916. Unfortunately, where the

A local Toronto ball team heads off to another game.

photo was taken, the name of the team (a hint: there's a letter "F" on the sweaters), and even the kind of car (a huge son of a gun) all remain a mystery. Any ideas?

The second photo is obviously today's "Old" City Hall. With the Cenotaph in place the date must be after 1925, the year the empty

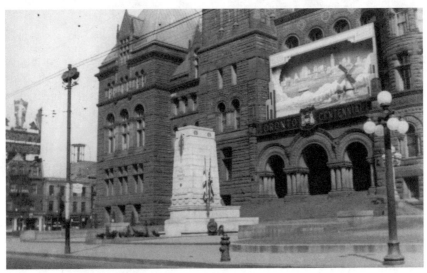

Toronto City Hall, 1934.

tomb (the origin of the word *cenotaph*) was dedicated. However, the real clue as to the actual date the photo was taken is the presence of the mural over the main entrance, on which are the words "Toronto Centennial." Bingo! Someone snapped this photo in 1934, the one-hundredth anniversary year of the city's incorporation.

The third photo shows a submarine moored at the foot of York Street with the old Terminal Warehouse (now the beautiful Queen's Quay Terminal) in the background. The vessel is the S-49, an American sub launched in 1921 in Bridgeport, Connecticut. The S-49 helped engineers develop future similar craft. However, in 1926, an accident onboard the experimental submarine resulted in the death of four of her crew members.

US submarine S-49 visiting Toronto, April 1938.

The vessel was subsequently repaired and continued in a variety of testing programs for the US Navy until decommissioned in 1936. It was then sold for scrap, but before being cut into pieces it was given a new life by a private individual who converted the craft into a tourist attraction.

In this view, S-49 is shown during its three-week visit to Toronto, during which anyone with twenty-five cents(children fifteen cents) could tour the craft.

When the United States entered the Second World War, S-49 was re-acquired and recommissioned, only to sink off the coast of Maryland in December 1942.

December 16, 2001

Exposing Our Past in Pictures

In last week's column I featured a few of the many photographs showing an earlier Toronto that people have sent to me during the past year. Unfortunately, in the majority of cases the person who took the photo and the date the view was snapped are unknown. Determining where and when these pictures were taken is all part of the fun.

Take the trio of images in this week's column, for instance. Each one arrived without identification. However, with some detective work at least part of the mystery surrounding each photo was, you should pardon the expression, exposed.

Take the photo of the gentleman in the uniform. I'm pret-

ty sure he's one of the guides stationed at the observation deck atop the Bank of Commerce Building at 25 King Street West. For many years after the bank's opening in 1931, a trip to its observation deck (at thirty-four stories above street level the highest in the British Commonwealth) was as popular as a visit to the CN Tower is today. Though the building still stands as Commerce Court North, the observation deck has been closed for years. Incidentally, I based my guess on a couple of things visible in the old photo: the insignia on the cap (under a magnifying glass, a stylized "B of C" logo) and the partial word "vators" (probably "Elevators") on the sign in the background.

The uniformed lady was a guide at Casa Loma. I remember someone telling me these young ladies weren't paid and made money by selling souvenir postcards to visitors to the castle. This card was signed by Shirley Winter. The date is unknown.

The third picture is reproduced from a slide and while seen here in black and white it is actually in colour. It shows the grandstand at the old

Dufferin Racetrack that was located on the west side of Dufferin Street, a site now occupied by the Dufferin Mall. It was one of several popular city racetracks, the others being Woodbine, Long Branch, and Thorncliffe Park. My guess is the picture was taken sometime in the 1940s.

Keep those old photos coming.

December 23, 2001

Tracing Toronto's Tracks

Last week's column featured a photograph of the old racetrack that stood on the west side of Dufferin Street just south of Bloor, right where the busy Dufferin Mall is located today. The track opened in 1908 and closed some forty-seven years later. Memories of the old track prompted reader Vera Mason, a long-time neighbour of both the racetrack and now the shopping centre, to send along her memories. Rather than paraphrase her letter, I'm reprinting it here for all to enjoy. The comments in square brackets are mine.

> I was born in 1920 in the front room of the house my father built in 1908 and in which I still live. It's almost directly behind the Dufferin Mall, which when I was born was old Abe Orpen's racetrack, popularly known as Dufferin Racetrack.
>
> When I was very young father used to take me to the circus which came to the track once a year. It was preceded by a circus parade that started at the old TTC car barns on Lansdowne [west side, just north of Bloor Street and now abandoned], turned east along Bloor, south on Brock and east again along Chesley into the track through one of the entrances.

Crowds at Dufferin (to many better known as Sufferin') Racetrack, 1937. Note Kent Public School near the Bloor and Dufferin intersection in the background.

We always got to see the parade, which was free, but couldn't often afford the performances. My older brother sometimes got in by helping to water the elephants. It was enough for me to see them walking in line each holding with his trunk the tail of the one ahead [a sight that prompts a very old joke that's too lengthy to tell here]. Visions of the big cats in their cages and the many clowns turning cartwheels along the route still remain vivid in my mind.

During the Depression years, Mother, Dad, and I often sat on the verandah on warm spring evenings and watched the betting crowd going home and tried, often in vain, to find a face looking as if its owner had won a couple of dollars. Mother would say, "Looks like they don't have two nickels to rub together," to which Dad invariably replied "They have high hopes, though" or "It's probably the only pleasure they have."

One of the main players at Dufferin (and Long Branch and Thorncliffe) racetracks, the ubiquitous Abe Orpen.

In my teens I learned to ride a bicycle around the track [half-mile] and when I attended Central Commerce the school held its athletic meets there.

About 1955 the mall people bought the property and for a time it was used for different kinds of entertainment. One summer it featured a theatre-in-the-round [Melody Fair] and I could sit on my kitchen windowsill and sing along to *Oklahoma!*, *Brigadoon*, and *Annie Get Your Gun*.

In 1957 they started to tear down the grandstand and stables. My two small sons watched from the windows and when the demolition crew started John would call, "Mom they're swingin' the big ball."

One day when they started on the stables Bertie came running in from the yard to tell me there was a "big thing" there. I went over and found a huge stable rat, at least as big as a large alley cat, peering into a hole by the hydro pole at the back fence at the bottom of our garden. I grabbed a rock and pinned him in the hole. As my husband was out of town and not knowing what else to do I called the police [at old #7 Station on Ossington]. "No problem ma'am, we'll look after it for you." An officer soon came by and seeing the situation let the rat out of the hole and promptly shot it. [Imagine doing that today!] I was a little disconcerted to see the officer then pick the creature up by the tail and drop it into my garbage can. However,

DUFFERIN

3 P.M.

TODAY AND

TOMORROW

AND EVERY DAY JUNE 4 - 11

Admission (Including Tax) $1.20   Children Under Sixteen Not Admitted

EXCELLENT LUNCH COUNTER

A 1947 newspaper ad for Dufferin Track.

I was too grateful to say anything but "thanks."

A little later, about 1960, a strip plaza opened on the site. It was very convenient for shopping. No longer did I have to walk up to Bloor or down to College or Dundas.

In 1972 the plaza became an enclosed mall as it is now. The young people there are amazed when I tell them it was once a racetrack and I was there.

Thanks for the memories, Vera.

December 30, 2001

Fort York Under Attack

During the twenty-six years I have been writing this column I have received a wide variety of questions on the subject of Toronto's fascinating past. One of the most frequent questions is which of Toronto's few remaining city landmarks is the most historic. As the term "historic" has a number of meanings, the question obviously has a number of answers. In my opinion the complex of structures now known as Fort York is number one, especially when it comes to understanding the story behind the evolution of our community from a military outpost set in a forest environment to the modern, energetic city we know and cherish today. In fact, I don't think it would be stretching a point to make the same statement relative to the entire Greater Toronto Area.

To be historically accurate, Fort York was originally known simply as the Garrison at York (York being our community's name until it was changed to Toronto in 1834). The term Fort York is a much more recent title and reflects attempts to make the site more tourist-friendly.

Throughout the garrison's 209 years, it has often been faced with destruction. The first such attempt occurred during the infamous thirty-month-long War of 1812, when invading forces from south of the border attempted to conquer our young nation, a calamity that would have forced us all to turn and salute the Stars and Stripes. During the conflict several attacks were made on the small Town of York, as well as on the garrison. The fort was severely damaged and was partially

Fort York's cannons appear ready to do battle should the new Gardiner Expressway get too close, *circa* 1960.

rebuilt after the war. As the years passed the buildings were allowed to deteriorate, and soon the historic site became an eyesore.

In 1903 the city acquired both the fort and the adjacent Garrison Common from the federal government for a mere $200,000. The city was particularly eager to get the Common so that expansion of the grounds of the popular Toronto Industrial Exhibition (now the CNE) could proceed. Part of the deal was an understanding that the city would restore the fort.

Even with this safeguard in place, it wasn't long before the city fathers were busily endorsing a plan that would see a streetcar line constructed right through the middle of the fort — in order, it was said, to permit easier access to the fairgrounds. Once again, Fort York was under threat. Fortunately, the day was saved when a by-law to allow the expenditure of funds for the new line was defeated by the electorate. With no thanks to the custodians of our city's history, the fort's historic buildings were spared.

Nevertheless, a new line was constructed from a point on Bathurst Street, south of the steam railway tracks, westerly to the Exhibition's east entrance. The new streetcar tracks followed a course next to the fort's north ramparts, and while some damage was done, this project was far less destructive than the original concept.

The city fathers didn't get around to restoring the fort until someone proposed the idea as part of Toronto's centennial celebrations, which were held in 1934. Much work had to be done, and fortunately, with so many out of work due to the Great Depression, workers came cheap. On Victoria Day of 1934, "Historic Fort York" opened to the public.

But the site, one of the most historic in the country, still had its enemies, though this time they weren't from south of the border — they were from City Hall.

In 1958, when the proposed cross-waterfront expressway was still in the planning stages, several Metro Toronto councillors, led by domineering Metro Chairman Fred Gardiner (whose name would ultimately be attached

This giant billboard shows the size of one of the many condo towers that, if approved, will be built along Fleet Street directly south of the fort.

to the roadway), insisted that a portion of the elevated structure be constructed over the fort. Someone even suggested that to keep the fort "authentic," it should be moved back to the water's edge where it had been located originally. The fact that extensive landfilling over the decades had made the fort appear to have moved inland was apparently lost. Ultimately, saner heads prevailed, and again the fort's integrity was preserved.

Today, the future of Fort York, a declared national historic site, is once again in jeopardy. If developers have their way, a row of condominium towers reaching twenty-six to thirty-six storeys into the sky will be constructed along Fleet Street directly south of the fort. Eventually, hemmed in by railway tracks to the north and by a wall of buildings to the south, there's little doubt that what the invaders from the States attempted to accomplish in 1813 may soon become a fact. The fate of one of our national treasures is in the hands of the Ontario Municipal Board. Its decision is imminent.

January 6, 2002

---

* Despite concerns expressed by a wide variety of opponents, the OMB approved the project.

Streetwalkin' Man

An interesting way to learn about our city's past is to become a streetwalker. Now, there are two kinds of streetwalkers, and before I get into real trouble, the one I'm talking about doesn't do it professionally. My kind of streetwalker roams the city streets with only one purpose in mind: to search out relics and remnants of days gone by. To accomplish this goal, the more successful of this particular brand of streetwalker uses a special trick (sorry, wrong choice of word) ... he or she looks up, above the modern storefronts, where one can often find signs, carvings, and other clues to an earlier Toronto.

All too often, the origins of these "treasures" won't be immediately evident, and some detective work will have to be done. A case in point is the date carved high over the fourth-floor corner window on the "ancient" structure at the northwest corner of Yonge and Temperance streets in the heart of the city. The year 1897 is obviously the date the building was erected. But who built it, and what was it used for?

To answer those questions a search through old City of Toronto directories, which can be found at the City Archives (on Spadina Road just south of Casa Loma) or in one of the public libraries where such resource material is kept on hand, came up with the following data. The building, listed in the old books as 140-42 Yonge Street, was the showroom and factory of W. & D. Dineen Co., retailers of "hats, caps and fine furs."

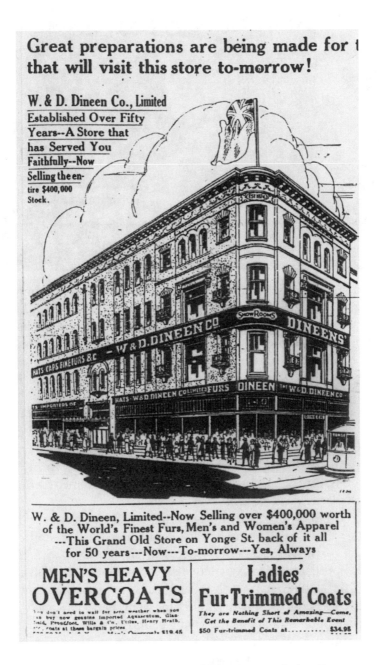

W. & D. Dineen ad from a 1924 edition of the *Evening Telegram* newspaper. Though ground level changes have been made to the old building, many elements of the 1897 structure are still evident in the modern-day photo.

Expanding my search, I found a lengthy history of the company in another important resource book in the library, *The Toronto Board of Trade, A Souvenir Edition.* This massive work, which was published in 1893, four years before the Dineen enterprise moved to the Yonge and Temperance location, reveals the following story.

The initials W and D stood for brothers William and Dennis Dineen, the latter having started the company in the 1870s. He had passed away long before the company relocated from 76 Yonge (at King) to 140-42 Yonge in 1897. William, the younger brother, was born in Ireland in 1838 and came with the rest of the Dineen family to Toronto the following year, a mere five years after the Town of York became the City of Toronto. After his schooling he joined Dennis, and when the latter died, he took over the business.

The company grew rapidly, requiring a move to a new and larger building at Temperance Street. Dineen purchased seal and other skins from sources in Russia, Persia, Germany, and Austria, with the raw goods shipped to Toronto, where the company's talented craftsmen fashioned them into hats, caps, robes, cloaks, and coats here in this old building. These much-sought-after items were then sold locally as well as through outlets all across the young country.

Continuing my search through a succession of directories revealed that the company stayed at the Temperance corner until 1928. The company then disappears from the listings, and one wonders whether the Great Depression finally did them in. There is no definitive answer to that question.

A couple more local history books have recently come to my attention, and while they were too late to be included on my holiday gift list, all three are worth adding to your Toronto history library. Of special interest to those who grew up in the Bloor and Bathurst part of our city (as I did) is a dandy new book by Ted Schmidt that'll bring back memories of the old neighbourhood. Remember St. Peter's Catholic Church on Bathurst north of Bloor and the school on the other side of the street south of Bloor? And the Midtown, Alhambra, and Bloor theatres, old Bathurst Street United Church and its tenant, the popular Midtown K-Club? And what about the popular playground not far from the Harbord and Bathurst intersection? And who could forget the ball games at Christie Pits, the Markus brothers, and some guy named Ed Mirvish who opened a small clothing store at Bloor and Markham streets (wonder what ever happened to Ed?). Ted's book, *Shabbes Goy, a Catholic Boyhood on a Jewish Street in a Protestant Toronto*, is available for $21.95 from Broughton's Gifts, 2105 Danforth Avenue, phone 416 690-4777.

Moving on to an another part of Toronto, John Gell has recently reprinted his book *Memories of Lambton Park*, in which he traces the history of the community that developed in and around Dundas Street and the Humber River from the time it was first settled in the late 1700s through to the 1950s. John's 235-page book, complete with more than 150 rare old photos, is available for $25 from the author by calling 416-769-2298.

January 13, 2002

Glory Days of the Palace Pier

Sharp-eyed readers will have noticed the presence of a brief tag line at the end of this column that promos the fact that each Friday morning I chat briefly with AM740's morning show hosts Tom Fulton and Mary Feely on the anniversary of some event from Toronto's past.

Now, for those who haven't yet had the pleasure of discovering the station, one important component of AM740's music format (in addition to the music of the 1950s and early '60s) is the sounds of the big bands. With this in mind, I though it especially appropriate for me to talk about the start of construction of one of the country's most popular dance halls, the Palace Pier. That construction began exactly seventy-one years (and a couple of hours) prior to my chat with Tom and Mary, when the obligatory cornerstone of the first building in the proposed four-building complex was tapped into place by former Canadian prime minister Arthur Meighen.

Though faced with a succession of obstacles, once the Palace Pier got up and running it would be home to virtually every major American

The Palace Pier as it might have been, 1927.

What Torontonians actually got, *circa* 1940.

dance band (with the exception of that of Glenn Miller, who performed here only once at the arena on Mutual Street) before the ill-starred structure was destroyed by flames in early 1963. The Palace Pier and Palace Place condos now tower over the site.

Because of radio's unshakeable time constraints I was only able to present the briefest of stories during my visit on AM740. The full story of the fascinating Palace Pier is presented here.

The idea of a major amusement pier for Toronto, one similar to those scattered throughout England, was first put forward by its promoters in the summer of 1927. The pier would feature four major structures: a 260-foot-long year-round ballroom at the mainland end, followed by a 240-foot-long Palace of Fun, a 170-foot-long bandstand, and a 1,500-seat theatre.

These buildings, plus several walkways and promenades, would stretch nearly a third of a mile out into Lake Ontario. To permit access by water, several lake boat wharfs would flank both sides of the pier.

Ads in the city's daily newspapers offered the public shares, at $10 each, in a company that would both build and operate this $1.5-million project. Reading between the lines of the company prospectus, it's obvious that investors were enticed using suggestions that a nice profit was virtually guaranteed once the new pier was up and running. After all, read the document, wasn't Toronto "a major tourist destination with nearly 3 million of the free-est spending visitors in the world"? And wasn't an amusement pier "the greatest of all-year-round amusement enterprises"? And wasn't Toronto's to be a "pier without peer"? Obviously, investors couldn't lose.

Initially, it was suggested that the eighteen-hundred-foot-long project be built either at Kew Beach or south of High Park, near the foot of Parkside Drive. However, no deal could be struck with the landlords, the Toronto Harbour Commissioners, and the developers decided to move further west (the Harbour Commission's jurisdiction ended at the Humber River), eventually opting for a site outside Toronto at the mouth of the Humber River in what was then the Township of Etobicoke.

It obviously took a while for a large enough portion of the investment money to be subscribed, since it wasn't until early 1931 that work on the first building, the ballroom, got underway. As it would turn out, this would be the only structure built.

Next, the company became embroiled in a number of lawsuits, including one with the province when a new alignment of the Lakeshore Road cut off the approaches to the pier.

More than a decade passed before the abbreviated Palace Pier finally opened, not as a dance hall, but as the Strathcona Palace Pier roller rink (an "annex" to the Strathcona rink uptown on Christie Street). The first celebrity roller skater was Bob Hope who, on June 18, 1941, took the opportunity to both skate and flog his new film, *Caught in the Draft*, which had just arrived in town.

It took a while for the big bands to find the place, but when they did the Palace Pier quickly became the city's pre-eminent dance hall. Then came the wrestlers, the boxers (George Chuvalo fought his first fight at the Pier), and the "Grand Old Opry."

But, on January 7, 1963, it all came to an end when an arsonist turned what remained of a once spectacular dream into a funeral pyre.

January 20, 2002

Bridging the Gap

Here's a little Toronto trivia with which to dazzle your friends. How many bridges are there in Toronto? No, not the kind you obtain from your friendly dentist, but rather the kind that you drive (or walk) over or under during your daily travels around town.

Give up? Well, there's a total of approximately five hundred bridges in the city.

Historically, the earliest bridges in and around our community were those over the lower portions of both the Don and Humber rivers. Research indicates that soon after the Town of York was established in 1793, a "bridge" of sorts was created over the Don by aligning a fallen log in such a way as to afford passage for those on foot over the clear, flowing waters of the meandering watercourse. (The Don didn't take its present shape until the late nineteenth century, when it was straightened in hopes of having sailing vessels load and unload at berths located as far north as Gerrard Street.)

As the years went by, other structures were erected over the Don, most of which were quickly destroyed when the river flooded each spring. One of the best known was Scadding's Bridge, located where the Kingston Road (now Queen Street) crossed the river. This rudimentary structure got it's name from the nearby Scadding property, on which stood the little Scadding cabin that many years later was moved to its present location on the CNE grounds.

Work began on erecting a new bridge over the Don River in July 1922. It was ready for traffic in mid-December of the following year.

In 1808, some civic-minded citizens contributed enough money to erect a more substantial structure. The need for contributions arose because taxation of personal real estate to raise funds for municipal public works and the like was still almost 20 years in the future. This particular bridge was only in use for a few years before it was destroyed in late April 1813 by British forces as they fled the town following the capture of Fort York by American troops.

A series of new bridges was constantly being erected over the river, with each in turn being destroyed by spring floods that would scour the river valley, often carrying the newest Queen Street bridge out into Toronto Bay.

Eventually, city officials decided that what was really necessary was a "high level" structure, with footings and road bed well away from the roaring spring flood water. Work began on this new bridge in October 1910, and it was completed almost exactly one year later. This structure still forms the main component of the present Queen Street East bridge over the Don.

Two bridges north of the Queen bridge is the one at Gerrard Street. There's been a bridge in this general vicinity since the mid-1850s. Back then, however, it would have been known by another name since the narrow dirt thoroughfare running eastward out of the young city was

Same view, 2002.

still called Don Street. This street, which was eventually incorporated into the Gerrard thoroughfare as the city grew in size, crossed the river via a small wooden structure. On the east side of the river it connected with another dirt road known as the Don and Danforth Road.

In 1893, the wooden structure (which had also been bruised and battered by the Don in flood) was replaced by an iron bridge. This more substantial structure allowed the streetcars on the recently electrified Carlton route to be extended from Sword Street to Pape Avenue. In July 1922, this structure, built at a cost of $700,000, was replaced by the present Gerrard Street,which reopened to streetcar traffic on December 16, 1923.

January 27, 2002

Toronto, A Safe Haven

One of the most famous photographs to ever appear in the late, lamented *Toronto Telegram*, a newspaper that served generations of readers from its inception on April 18, 1876, until its final edition hit the streets on October 30, 1971, was snapped in 1942 in front of Union Station by the paper's talented news photographer, Nels Quarrington.

That photo showed a burly city policeman welcoming a young war guest, Simon Christopher Dew, to a new life out of harm's way here in Toronto. Master Dew was one of the hundreds of children who found a safe haven here in Canada far away from the enemy bombers that continued to pound cities and towns throughout Great Britain.

The police officer in the photo was six-foot-three Constable Harry Wharton, who, in his bobby-like uniform with helmet, must have looked very much like the policemen Simon knew back home. As it would turn out, the youngster liked Toronto so much he eventually returned, and when I last spoke with him, he was living in the Cabbagetown part of our city.

Throughout the rest of the war, Quarrington's photo was used in numerous fundraising projects and in doing so helped a variety of organization's amass more than $3 million, much of which was used to assist in bringing other British children to safety here in Canada.

When I came across the photograph during my frequent searches through the old *Telegram* newspaper, now captured on microfilm in the

Toronto Police Constable Harry Wharton welcomes war guest Christopher Dew to our city, 1942.

Toronto Sun's News Research Centre, it prompted the second photograph that accompanies this column.

During my stint in the employ of the Canadian National Exhibition (an obvious career choice following my three-year education in

Constable Mike Sale greets a young CNE visitor in Centennial Square, 1979. Mike joined the force in 1971 and has recently retired after more than thirty years of service to our city.

Chemical Technology at Ryerson), I became the fair's Centennial Projects Manager and worked on a number of things that were intended to recognize the CNE's one-hundredth anniversary in 1978. (To show how time flies, in just two fairs from now the Ex will celebrate its 125th!)

One of the major projects to make the Exhibition of 1978 special was the construction of Centennial Square at the west end of the grounds. Here, the sights and sounds of a small Canadian community at the turn of the century were presented to CNE visitors. The square had things like a replica of the original bandstand, a candy store, an ice cream shop, a movie theatre, an ancient streetcar, and, of course, a policeman on patrol.

Our constable was a real, live Metro Toronto policeman, Michael Sale, who was there to ensure law and order were maintained throughout Centennial Square. Constable Sale was outfitted in an authentic 1900s-ish uniform complete with a bobby helmet (in fact, Toronto city police wore bobby helmets until well after the end of the Second World War). To get the busy constable to all corners of the square, Mike had a patrol bicycle similar to those used on the streets of an earlier Toronto.

One day, as Constable Sale was on patrol, I saw him chatting with a young CNE visitor. The photo of Constable Wharton with the war guest flashed into my mind and I snapped the second photo seen here.

Over the years, Mike Sale and I have become good friends. And during that time he has proven to me (and to others) that there's no one who has more pride in Toronto's police force or knows more about its history than he does.

For many years Mike was the force's spokesperson and became well known to the media. His most recent accomplishment was the organization of what many regard as the most successful Chiefs of Police Conferences in the long history of that organization.

Recently, Mike decided to retire from the Toronto Police Service after more than thirty years as a cadet, constable, sergeant, staff sergeant, and, most recently, inspector.

A lot has happened in and to our city since Constable Sale patrolled Centennial Square those many years ago. But one thing remains certain. Our city is better place for having Mike Sale, and people like him, there to serve and protect. Thanks Mike, and have a happy and healthy retirement.

February 3, 2002

When the Leafs Budded

I don't know about you, but I'm pretty sure this is the year the Leafs are going to win the Stanley Cup. On the other hand, maybe they'll take it next year. You know, they really should'a taken it last year.

Ah, the undying loyalty of a Leafs fan. And you know you've been a Leafs fan for a long time when, in a group of people, you are the only one who can remember the last time the Leafs did win that blankety-blank Cup!

However, I figure that this season is the one simply because a very important anniversary in the team's long and illustrious history is about to occur. It's like two heavenly planets in conjunction. It just has to be. Well, that plus the fact that someplace called Hell has just frozen over.

It was exactly seventy-five years ago this coming Friday that the team that represented Toronto in the NHL played its first game under the name Toronto Maple Leafs.

Prior to February 15, 1927, the team was known as the Toronto St. Pats, though even this name was not its first. For year the boys had played as the Toronto Arenas in recognition of the fact that the team's home games were played in the arena on Mutual Street. (Many years later, the Mutual Street Arena was extensively remodelled and renamed The Terrace. It has since been torn down.)

The change in name from St. Pats to Maple Leafs took place soon after millionaire businessman Hugh Aird and his friend Conn Smythe bought the lacklustre team on February 15, 1927. In an effort to give the team a wider appeal, the owners decided that a more patriotic name was needed. The person who selected the name Maple Leafs was Smythe, who had fought in the Great War under the maple leaf insignia. In his eyes, the maple leaf was truly a symbol of Canada!

Smythe also felt that while there were already three Canadian teams in the ten-team NHL besides Toronto's St. Pats (the Canadiens and the Maroons from Montreal and the Senators from Ottawa — Smythe had some reservations about anything from Quebec representing Canada), there were twice as many teams representing the United States (the New York Americans and Rangers, the Detroit Cougars, the Boston Bruins, the Pittsburgh Hornets, and the Chicago Blackhawks). It was Smythe's plan to make his new Maple Leafs team not simply Toronto's favourite sports team, but the nation's favourite as well. With this new name perhaps he could attract more fans. With more fans, there'd be more income. With more income Smythe could afford better players. And with better players, who knows, maybe a Stanley Cup was not too far in the future. (The Leafs' first Stanley Cup did come in 1932 in Smythe's new 14,473-

The Arena Gardens on Mutual Street where the Arenas, the St. Pats, and, after February 15, 1927, the newly named Toronto Maple Leafs played hockey. The Leafs moved to the Gardens four years later.

(Above) That's Conn Smythe, back row, second from right. (Left) George Patterson in his later years. Patterson scored the Leafs' very first goal seventy-five years ago.

seat Maple Leaf Gardens, which had nearly doubled the seating capacity of the old Mutual Street Arena.)

There was just one problem with using the Maple Leafs in time for the February 15 game against Detroit. There was concern that legal problems might arise, since most of the Toronto players had been signed to a St. Pats contract at the beginning of the season. As a result, while the team's name had been changed to the Maple Leafs, officially it was still the St. Pats.

Checking through the papers, one sees that these two names are used interchangeably for the next few games. In fact, a newspaper ad for the February 19 game against the Maroons was still calling the team the St. Pats, while the news story about that very same game called them the Maple Leafs.

Nevertheless, most fans agree that the Toronto Maple Leafs' very first game under that name was the match against the New York Americans on February 17, 1927. And we won, 4–1.

The Toronto lineup consisted of John Ross Roach in goal, Day, Corbeau, Halderson, and Brydge on defence, and Bailey, McCaffery, Keeling, Voss, Patterson, and Dr. Bill Carson (yup, Dr. Carson) up front.

These last three players are of particular interest. Carl Voss (who became a referee and the NHL's first referee-in-chief) was the first player to be signed to a Toronto Maple Leafs contract, George Patterson scored the first Maple Leafs goal, and Bill Carson was a graduate of U of T's Academy of Dentistry and was quite a player with the university's team, the Dentals. Dr. Carson was born in Bracebridge in 1899, was varsity hockey team captain for two years, and helped win the Allan Cup in 1921. The good dentist passed away in Parry Sound in 1967.

My thanks to Dr. Anne Dale at the Academy of Dentistry for details about Dr. Carson. True Leafs fans would do well to pick up a copy of Andrew Podnieks's book *The Essential Blue and White Book* (Douglas & McIntyre). It has everything you ever wanted to now about our Leafs, who are about to win their twelfth Stanley Cup. Or was that next year?

February 10, 2002

On the Shelf

A while ago I received a large collection of old photos and negatives from a reader in Barrie. They were in a trunk that was owned by an elderly gentleman who had recently passed away. My new-found friend in Barrie offered the collection to me, as the owner had no family.

Several of the photos were of Toronto parades, sporting events on the Island and in local playgrounds, and waterfront scenes. These were certainly keepers. The negatives, on the other hand, had not been looked after properly, and most had deteriorated badly. A few, however, looked salvageable, so I took them to Charles Abel's Photofinishing at the foot of Sherbourne StreetStreet. Irene at the front desk said that she would see what could be done with them. When I returned a week or so later I was presented with a dozen prints from negatives that I had been sure were totally useless. I'll let you see some of those prints in future columns. It all goes to prove that old negatives should not be discarded simply because they look old. There may be some treasures just waiting to be liberated.

The print I selected to feature in today's column took a little detective work to identify. A couple of clues helped me deduce that the view depicts the intersection of Bay and Adelaide streets in the heart of downtown Toronto. The distinctive shape of the streetcar at the top left of the view is that of one of the TTC's so-called "large" Peter Witts, which operated on the Bay route. It's stopped opposite the popular

Looking down on the Bay and Adelaide intersection, *circa* 1947.

Savarin hotel and restaurant (at 336-44 Bay Street). The office building a little further south at the Adelaide corner is the dignified Northern Ontario Building, which is, mercifully, still there. It got its name from having been constructed at a time when the mineral riches of the "New" Ontario to the north were being discovered in great quantities. Many of the offices in the building were occupied by mining companies. Note also the traffic on Adelaide is still travelling in both directions. Adelaide and Richmond were made one-way in 1958.

Could the lack of traffic mean the photo was taken on a Sunday?

As to the actual month and year the picture was taken, the shadows in the view establish that it must have been snapped one afternoon in the spring or summer. As to the year, a clue can be found at the bottom of the photo. That large hole is being excavated for the new $2-million Woolworth Building that officially opened at the southeast corner of the intersection on November 30, 1949, or so a three-page ad in the *Telegram* newspaper told me. What that same ad didn't tell me is just when construction of the structure began. With the shortage of steel that prevailed following the end of the Second World War (delaying the opening of the Toronto-Barrie Highway, now 400, and a variety of other major steel-dependent projects) the Woolworth structure was probably under construction for a longer period of time than normal. I'll guess the date as the spring or fall of 1947. Anyone know for sure?

Woolworth Building, Toronto, Canada

A postcard view of Toronto's Woolworth Building at the southeast corner of Bay and Adelaide. The postmark dates the day the card was sent as August 31, 1951.

The Woolworth structure didn't make it to its first half-century mark, having been torn down several years ago, with the valuable site used as a parking lot ever since. Recently however, it was announced that a new hotel/condominium complex soaring sixty-five storeys over the nation's financial heart is soon to be erected on the corner. To be known as the Ritz-Carlton, it will be a $200-million project, with the opening scheduled for the year 2004.

February 17, 2002

* The project has been renamed Trump International Hotel and Tower.

Tripping Down Gasoline Alley

With the various problems associated with gasoline-powered vehicles, we hear more and more these days about alternate-fuel vehicles. All over the world people are working on cars and trucks powered by such things as compressed natural gas, ethanol, various fuel cells, electricity from nickel methyl hydride batteries — and the list goes on. Who knows, the ultimate winner may be something no one has even considered.

Here in Toronto, the idea of a horseless carriage operating on something other than gasoline was very much on the minds of true automobile enthusiasts. In fact, the *Toronto Daily Star* published an Automobile Supplement in one of its July 1901 newspapers. In it there was a column titled "How Autos Are Propelled," in which the author reported on a total of six different kinds of automobile propulsion systems then in use or development: gasoline, electricity, steam, compressed air, carbonic acid gas, and alcohol. The story went on to report that someone had recently connected a small eight-horsepower gasoline engine to an electrical generator, which in turn supplied current to an on-board storage battery, thus rendering the vehicle independent of a "charging station." Sound familiar? That combination is the basic principle behind today's Honda and Toyota hybrids.

One of the pioneers in the use of an electric-powered automobile was a young Toronto patent attorney, Frederick Barnard Fetherstonhaugh. In the fall of 1896, Fetherstonhaugh arranged to have a city electrician, one William Still, build him an "electric," the operation of which was described thus: the battery consisted of thirty-six cells weighing twenty-three pounds each, giving a maximum of about four horsepower. The cells were of the lead paste type, their average voltage about 1.9 for the entire discharge. The motor was of the disc armature type, six polar, the field being series wound. When the battery was fully charged it was estimated that it was capable of propelling the carriage about thirty miles without recharging. The total weight of the vehicle was 1,200 pounds, of which 750 pounds represented the electrical equipment.

Mr. Fetherstonhaugh's electric car on display at the Toronto Exhibition at the turn of the last century.

This one-of-a-kind vehicle, which was recharged each evening from the streetcar overhead outside Fetherstonhaugh's Lake Shore Road residence, was built in Still's factory at 710-24 Yonge Street and actually saw service for almost fifteen years. It was a special feature at the annual Toronto Exhibition (now CNE) on several occasions until, like many of our historic artifacts, it just up and disappeared.

William Still went on to manufacture a variety of other electric vehicles in his factory before being bought out by British capitalists who ran the company under the name Canadian Motors Ltd. The company was initially very successful and began supplying the lucrative British market. Unfortunately, and for a variety of reasons, the company went broke in late 1902.

Simpson's charcoal-burning delivery truck in front of the company's Mail Order Building on Mutual Street (now condos), September 1943.

A few years later, a new company, Canada Cycle and Motor, took over the Yonge Street factory, in which it produced a new "electric" called the Ivanhoe. CCM eventually moved to west Toronto, where the company began manufacturing the Russell, the nation's first financially successful homegrown gasoline-powered automobile.

Over the next few years it became evident that the big oil interests were out to ensure that what had initially been a useless by-product of the distillation process, something called gasoline, would be the automobile fuel of the future. Once that happened there was little or no reason to search for other sources of energy. That is, until the outbreak of the Second World War. Oil and gasoline were soon in short supply, and gas and tire rationing went into effect.

For many, trips in the family car had to be curtailed, while businesses that relied on deliveries were even harder hit. They had to come up with other ways to deliver their goods. Many bakeries and dairies reverted to delivering milk and bread by horse-drawn wagon, just as they had years earlier.

But there just weren't enough traffic-savvy horses to go around. So, in the fall of 1943, Toronto's Robert Simpson Company (which became part of The Bay in 1978) came up with a novel way to keep at least one of their trucks on the road while abiding by the stringent gasoline rationing regulations.

Company mechanics added a hopper and a charcoal burner to the rear of the vehicle, and prior to each day's deliveries, the hopper was filled. Some charcoal fell into the burner, where it was lit using a gasoline or oil wick. After about five minutes, the charcoal gas that was released was piped to the engine compartment, through the engine's throttle, and into the intake manifold, where it was ignited by the spark plugs. No carburetor was needed. Metal netting around the charcoal-burning unit kept inquisitive children safe.

During initial experiments, seventy pounds of charcoal (costing about $3.50) gave off charcoal gas equivalent to ten gallons of gasoline, enough for the delivery man to do his daily rounds. The truck could achieve forty miles per hour.

I have yet to discover whether the experiment was a success and whether other vehicles in the fleet were converted. Anyone know?

February 24, 2002

Last Movie Palace

As a kid growing up here in Toronto, I had a fabulous array of large moving-picture palaces to choose from. Right downtown — a trip made even more fun by a ride on the streetcar — were the Tivoli and Victoria, the first situated on the southeast corner of the Richmond and Victoria street intersection, the second on the southwest. Over on Bay Street, just behind the old Eaton's store, was the mammoth 2,400-seat Shea's Hippodrome. Just opposite the Eaton's store, on the east side of Yonge, was the slightly smaller Loew's, and north of it, the giant of them all, the 3,400-seat Imperial. Not quite so far downtown, on Carlton between Yonge Street and the Gardens, was the Odeon Carlton, which actually opened as the Odeon Toronto. This theatre has a special interest for me since that is where I took my wife-to-be on our first date. I even remember the movie that was playing: *Under the Yum-Yum Tree* starring Jack Lemmon and Carol Lynley. And when I got Yarmila home she gave me a glass of milk and a couple of cookies. Honest!

Toronto had other large picture palaces: the University on Bloor West and the Uptown on Yonge south of Bloor, in those days still just a single 2,700-seat theatre. Further up Yonge, steps north of the St. Clair corner, were the Hollywood and the Odeon Hyland. Near the city limits was another large Odeon theatre, the Fairlawn. In fact, the Odeon people had two other large picture palaces here in Toronto: the Odeon Danforth in the east end and the Odeon

202

Newspaper ad for the opening of the new Eglinton Theatre, April 2, 1936.

Humber way out the other end of the Bloor-Danforth streetcar line (there are those streetcars again).

Today, except for Loew's and the Imperial, which continue to survive not as movie houses but as live theatre venues (Loew's as the Elgin in the Ontario Heritage Foundation's Elgin Winter Garden Theatre Centre and the Imperial as the Canon Theatre), all of Toronto's impressive movie palaces have been levelled. All but one, that is, and it too seems to have its days numbered. What an awful way to celebrate a sixty-sixth birthday.

When the new 1,080-seat Eglinton Theatre, located on the north side of Eglinton Avenue, a few steps west of the still fairly quiet Avenue Road intersection, had its public opening on the evening of April 2, 1936, the newspapers rushed to extol its virtues. Described as the "Show Place of Toronto," the new theatre was "modern to the latest degree and as spacious as she is she could not begin to handle the crowds of curious movie fans who stood in line for hours waiting their turn to enter. Inside the lobby, over the entrance doors is a huge mirror and as each person walks across the lobby they break an electric beam, which starts a group of fountains to play. There is no balcony in the theatre, but there is a raised mezzanine at the rear for loge seats. Here customers are allowed to smoke and each chair has an individual ash tray. The ventilation sys-

Crowds clog Eglinton Avenue as they eagerly await the opening of the city's newest motion picture theatre, April 2, 1936.

tem worked perfectly and no discomfort was caused the non-smokers. One special feature of the theatre which was greatly admired at the opening was the comfort of the chairs. There is nothing to compare with them in any other Toronto movie house."

The first presentation at the new theatre was a "talkie'" title, *King of Burlesque*, which starred Warner Baxter, Alice Fay, and Jack Oakie. Admission prices ranged from 45 cents for the best seats to 25 cents for students. Not surprisingly, there were no special deals for seniors, and while no extras were charged on the student ticket, all others had to pay a few cents amusement tax.

The Eglinton was air-conditioned, not a unique situation in Toronto, but it was certainly one of only a handful of theatres with such an up-to-date amenity. What was unique in the theatre, however, was the fact that it was equipped with acoustical devices for patrons with hearing difficulties. This feature is of special significance today when one of the reasons given for the grand old theatre's possible closure in early April is its lack of facilities for the physically handicapped.

To learn more about the theatre and what some people are suggesting in an attempt to prevent the loss of another city landmark, visit www.mikecolle.com.

March 3, 2002

The "Déjà Vu" from Here

Throughout history there have been numerous examples of "what ifs." For instance, what if the *Titanic* had hit that massive iceberg head-on instead of a glancing blow? Would the mighty ship have still gone to the bottom? And if it hadn't sunk, would anyone know or care about the *Titanic* today?

What if the planned invasion of Great Britain by the Germans during the early part of the Second World War had gone ahead and been successful? Would German have been my first language, and English my second?

Closer to home, what if the War of 1812 (the one we didn't start and didn't lose) had ended differently, with the American occupation of Upper and Lower Canada being permanent? Would winter stays in Florida by Canadians be cheaper?

Would there be another TTC fare increase if Lastman had stayed a refrigerator salesman?

In fact, one can speculate on how just about everything we take for granted today could have been so much different had things in the past taken a different turn.

What brings this fascinating concept of "what if" to mind is reading a wonderful new book on the Avro Arrow by Randall Whitcomb (ISBN 1-55125-082-9, Vanwell Publishing Ltd.).

While the story of the birth and death of this famous (or infamous,

The debut of the Arrow on October 4, 1957, was a remarkable event in the distinguished, yet all too short, history of Avro Canada.

depending on who you talk to) Canadian-designed all-weather super-sonic interceptor has been the subject of numerous books, films, videos, and web sites, the author expands on why the Arrow was never to be. Whitcomb goes much further in his new book and investigates what the future of this project, as well as many other projects proposed by the builder, Avro Canada, might have been had the government chosen not to end it all on February 20, 1959.

As the author acknowledges early in the book, many details on Avro Canada's past, present, and truncated future were supplied to him by the legendary Jim Floyd, who was, in many ways, the "father" of both the Jetliner (the world's first successful jet passenger aircraft) and the Arrow. It's Jim's wealth of knowledge about these and other company initiatives (knowledge that could not be destroyed in the same way that most of the drawings, plans, and in fact the Arrows themselves were expunged by government decree) that prompt the reader of this book to wonder "what if."

Here's an example. The trio of prototype Arrows that actually flew met and in some cases exceeded a variety of performance expectations.

Artist/author Randall Whitcomb's painting of the proposed CF-105 Arrow Mark 4.

This was in spite of having less powerful British-built engines installed as "interim" powerplants while the more powerful Avro Orenda engines were being perfected. Orenda-powered craft never got off the ground. What if ...?

Had the government not interfered (for reasons yet to be officially and unequivocally confirmed), a succession of improved Arrows already on the drawing boards, including the Mark 4 version (complete with ramjets), could have followed. Other plans were underway for an aircraft that would take travellers into space. This latter project was identified as Avro Canada's Space Threshold Vehicle. On February 20, 1959, these projects also died. What if ...?

But not all of Avro Canada's eggs were in one basket. When the end came that "Black Friday," some company personnel were investigating the relatively new fields of automation and computation in relation to the aircraft manufacturing industry, while others were assigned to nuclear and anti-gravity projects. Some were studying new and unusual materials for use in high-temperature situations.

Of particular interest to today's airport travellers (and especially following the Transport Minister's recent assertion that there will be a passenger link connecting downtown Toronto with Pearson Airport) was Avro's proposal to develop a turbine-powered monorail rapid transit system that could connect Toronto with Malton Airport (Malton being Pearson's original name). Interestingly, when the end came minutes after the scrapping of the Arrow more than forty-two years ago, this particular project was being touted as an undertaking (no pun intended) that could keep Avro Canada alive.

Another "what if" ...

There's another new book in the stores that also interests me, though for very different reasons. *The CHUM Story* by Allen Farrell (ISBN 0-7737-6263-9, Stoddart) covers the early years of a local radio station on whose newscast I would have learned the latest about Avro's fascinating collection of new aircraft: the Jetliner, the CF-100, and the Arrow. It's also where I first heard the music of some guy named Elvis Presley and where the talented Crew Cuts, the Diamonds, and the Four Lads proved that Canadians (and Torontonians at that) could also make it big on the Chum Charts. Farrell's book traces the history of the station from its inception in 1945 through the rock and roll years, up to and including the nation's wild and fun-filled centennial year of 1967. As familiar as the music was, so too were the station's DJs. Just reading names like Al Boliska, Duff Roman, John Spragge, and Bob "Night Train" Laine takes me back to hard studying at NTCI, chips and gravy at Theodore's, and Phil and Joan Lewis's little green Nash Metropolitan. A great read!

March 17, 2002

TD Centre on Horizon

People often find old pictures taken in and around our city, and every once in a while I'm asked to try to date the photos. To do so, I have to become a sort of Sherlock Holmes, searching for clues hidden within the image: things like a store name on a sign or awning, partial or full street names or numbers, and the presence of streetcar tracks, shadows, or a car or group of cars with, hopefully, licence plates showing. In this latter case, however, be careful. There are car buffs who will jump up and down if a 1936 car is in a photo identified as being from 1934. Nevertheless, a few of these leads combined with an examination of several old city directories found at the City Archives or some reference libraries will help identify where the picture was taken and, in some cases, when.

Now that's often a lot of work, but it is very rewarding when the clues result in an answer to the mystery. Some of the easiest photos to identify in general terms are those snapped of the skyline from the Island or from the deck of one of the city's ferry boats. In this case, the presence (or non-presence) of a prominent downtown building on the city skyline will help identify, in general terms at least, when the photo was taken.

Interestingly, the look of Toronto's skyline early in the last century can be broadly defined as pre-Royal York Hotel (topped off in early 1929) followed by a small window of time prior to the Bank of Commerce being completed less than two years later. This 34-storey, 476-foot-high build-

209

The arrival on the skyline of the first phase of the TD Centre, which was designed by John B. Parkin Associates and Bregman and Hamann partnership with Mies van der Rohe as consultant, was a defining moment in Toronto's financial and architectural history. Note early Toronto skyscrapers Royal York Hotel and Bank of Commerce in both views.

ing dominated the city skyline for more than three decades, and for most of that time it was proudly described as the tallest building not just here in Toronto, nor just in Canada, but in the entire British Commonwealth as well.

In 1962, our city suffered a couple of setbacks in the race to host the country's tallest structures when the CIBC Building and Place Ville Marie opened. What was worse, both buildings were located in Toronto's rival city, Montreal.

That city's claim to fame wasn't to last very long, for on November 6, 1962, just a few months after Montreal assumed the title "skyscraper capital of Canada," the TD Bank and land developer Cemp Investments Ltd. (established in 1951 by industrialist Samuel

BANK OF TORONTO, HEAD OFFICE BUILDING, TORONTO, CANADA.

One wonders whether this city landmark, the 1912 Bank of Toronto, should have, or indeed could have, been saved.

Bronfman and named for his four children, Charles, Edgar, Minda, and Phyllis) announced that together they would redevelop a six-acre site in downtown Toronto. The first phase would consist of a 55- to 60-storey building and an adjacent banking hall. More structures would come as the $100-million project unfolded over the next few years. Some said, "take that Montreal." This was one-upmanship at its best.

More than three years passed before the public got their first look at what the initial phase of their new TD Centre would look like. The main building, a soaring rectangular black glass slab, would be fifty-five storeys in height and would sit on a seven-acre site that would feature landscaped walkways and a pool. Nearby there'd be a three-storey banking hall also in black glass. Underground would feature shops and restaurants and two levels of parking.

Then, depending on the demand for additional office space, a second tower of forty storeys would be added. This tower, it was hoped, would serve as the new home of the Toronto Stock Exchange. This would result in the Exchange's elegant 1936 structure being demolished. Toronto would also lose the gracious 1912 Bank of Toronto building at the southwest corner of Bay and King streets. Judging from the reports in the newspapers of the day, no one seemed to care about the loss of these two old structures.

As it would turn out, the temple-like bank building would vanish while the graceful Toronto Stock Exchange building was left alone. Unfortunately, the old Exchange Building (now the Design Centre) is in trouble once again as plans evolve to disfigure its elegant art deco facade with the installation of huge showroom-type windows.

Work on the original TD Centre tower began with the official groundbreaking ceremony in June 1964. The building reached the halfway point a little more than a year later and was "topped off" in April 1966; the first tenants began arriving in March 1967. The official opening ceremony was held on May 13, 1968, and was presided over by Ontario Premier John Robarts, who had unveiled the project a little more than four years earlier.

The nearby banking pavilion, positioned on the site of the 1912 bank, opened to the public in the fall of 1968. The nearby forty-six-storey tower was completed a little more than a year later.

In December 2000, the TD Centre (which now comprises five buildings) was purchased by Cadillac Fairview, one of North America's largest investors, managers, and owners of commercial real estate. CF is wholly owned by the Ontario Teachers' Pension Plan Board.

March 24, 2002

Moving Story of Historic Home

Now here's a scary thought. Suppose for a moment that I owned Casa Loma or any other structure deemed to be of historic or architectural significance in this province. Did you know that, provided I follow the steps outlined in the Ontario Heritage Act, I have the unquestioned right to demolish that structure and to heck with you or anyone else who thinks it should be kept?

To be sure, there are a couple of hoops that this same act will make me go through in an attempt to keep the designated structure from being turned into a pile of rubble. Things like a 270-day waiting period (180 days plus an additional 90 days, if requested). It's during this period of time that interested parties are expected to discuss the possibility of keeping the place standing. In addition, here in Toronto at least, it's necessary that a permit for the project that will occupy the site of the heritage structure be approved before demolition can proceed. Unfortunately, this latter step is more of a formality than anything else. If the discussions come to nothing and the new project is approved, the fate of the old building is sealed.

In some cases the 270-day discussion period results in the developer recognizing the value of retaining the threatened building in total as a valuable component of the new project. A good example of this is the continued presence of the 1885 Bank of Montreal as part of the Hockey Hall of Fame in the BCE Place complex.

213

The old Campbell House sits at the top of Frederick Street awaiting its fate, 1971.

Thirty years ago today, Campbell House was nearing its final safe haven on the Canada Life lawn at the northwest corner of Queen and University. First, though, it had to spend a night sitting in the intersection. Final placement was done the next day, Easter Sunday, April 1, 1972.

On the other hand, such discussions may result in an agreement to save only parts of the heritage structure, which usually show up as facades glued onto the fronts of some of the new buildings in the development.

All too often, however, rescue attempts fail altogether and the building is demolished, lost forever.

I should mention that there are a couple of other possibilities. Local authorities (or some angelic organization) could buy the threatened building using money from a variety of sources, all of which normally lead back to the taxpayer's pocket. But with priorities like the feeding and sheltering of the homeless that idea becomes less and less feasible. Besides, many taxpayers couldn't care less about an "old" building, and politicians do have to get re-elected.

There's one more form of preservation, one that involves moving the threatened building to a safe and secure location. Many historians, as well as many history buffs, disagree with this practice. Without question, moving from its original site compromises the integrity of the heritage structure. However, given the lack of absolute protection under existing provincial laws, this action may be all that stands between keeping a building and just holding onto pictures and memories.

In fact, it was exactly thirty years ago today that a graceful, but grimy, old Toronto house was saved from demolition when it was moved more than a mile westward from its original site in the ancient York townsite to a new location on the northwest corner of the busy University and Queen intersection. There it rests today in safety, beautifully restored and protected by the good men and women of the Advocates' Society.

Campbell House was built in 1822 as the residence of Upper Canada's (now Ontario's) Chief Justice, Sir William Campbell. Its location on Duke Street, at the top of Frederick, allowed Sir William to live out his life with a clear view of the peninsula across the bay. A dozen years later the Town of York would be "erected" into the city we now know as Toronto.

Following the Chief Justice's death in 1834 (the same year York became Toronto) the house was used for a variety of purposes, including periods of time as a horse nail manufacturing plant, an elevator factory, and a warehouse. In its later years the building was owned by the Coutts Hallmark card people, and when this company decided it needed the space for a new building, instead of simply demolishing the old house (as the company had every right to do), the three-hundred-ton relic was sold to a group of trial lawyers, on the condition that the old building be moved. It was then that the Advocates' Society formed the Sir William Campbell Foundation and raised the necessary funds to move the house to the safety of the lawn south of the Canada Life building on University Avenue. The move, a world record in both size and distance, took place over the Easter weekend exactly thirty years ago this weekend.

Today the historic Campbell House serves as a meeting place for members of the Advocates' Society. In addition, it's open select hours for public tours.

March 31, 2002

Down Home Heroes

Today and tomorrow are special anniversary dates for the two people who appear in this column.

It was on this very day exactly twenty-five years ago (remember, it was a cold and snowy Thursday afternoon) that the gentleman described here hit the first ever home run in the history of major league baseball in Toronto. In fact, not only did rookie first baseman Doug Ault enter the history books by hitting the Blue Jay's first home run, but he also belted the team's second "round-tripper." Interestingly, Ault's first homer was over the left field fence at the now-demolished Exhibition Stadium, while his second sailed over the fence at right. In addition, Ault singled in the eighth inning, driving in the team's eighth run. The twenty-seven-year-old Ault had been claimed from the Texas Rangers in the third round of the expansion draft. His previous team had been Sacramento of the Pacific Coast minor league, where he had hit twenty-five home runs. The Jays went on to defeat the Chicago White Sox 9–5.

You know, I'll bet that more than half of those attending last Thursday's opener weren't even born when Ault made baseball history here in Toronto. Here are a few more opening day facts from quarter of a century ago (is it possible?). The pitcher that first game was Bill Singer (eleven hits in four innings); Toronto fielded two guys named Woods, Gary (centre field) and Alvin (right field); the game lasted 202 very cold minutes; and exactly 44,649 spectators attended the game,

217

most wrapped in blankets, fur coats, or snowmobile suits. Oh, and vendors weren't yet permitted to sell beer (so I assume nobody drank any).

Here's another almost forgotten fact from the team's earliest days. The team name, Blue Jays, wasn't a totally unanimous choice, not by a long shot. In fact, a "name the team" contest resulted in thirty thousand submissions, from which four thousand names were selected for consideration. A few that didn't make the cut were: Lumberjacks, Shamrocks, Mounties, "77s", Foresters, and someone (perhaps an Archie Bunker fan) even suggested Dingbats.

Amongst the other names considered, the colour blue predominated: Blue Bats (a play, perhaps, on Labatts, the team owner), Blue Sox, Blue Shoes, Blue Birds, and, of course, Blue Jays. In the official team history (*Blue Jays Album*, Seal Books, 1989) Peter Bavasi, the team's executive vice-president, confirmed that the name Blue Jays was selected because this species of bird is "indigenous to the Ontario region, it's feisty and aggressive, the kind of ball team we hope to field for the fans in Toronto."

By the way, the team lost its second game.

The second person of significance featured in this week's column appears in the two portraits, one showing her as a youngster, the other as the young women many senior readers will remember with great nostalgia. Strangely, however, while it's certain that tomorrow is, in fact, the anniversary of Gladys Marie Smith's birth, I'm really not sure whether it's the 109th or 110th. That's because when I requested data shown on her birth record (now on deposit at the Archives of Ontario), that official document revealed that she was born on April 8, 1892. This is in conflict with virtually every other reference to the

Toronto-born Gladys Smith became ...

218

... Mary Pickford, "America's Sweetheart."

young Toronto girl who grew up to be the world's first motion picture star, Mary Pickford. I hate to say it, but even the provincial plaque at the southwest corner of the Hospital for Sick children, site of her birthplace at 175 University Avenue, refers to her birth year as 1893.

The discrepancy may have been prompted by Mary's own attempt to retain the youthfulness that brought her worldwide fame on the silent movie screen by shortchanging herself by a year. Aside from this historical irregularity, there's no doubt that in her heyday "our Mary" (as most Canadians of the time referred to her) was the most famous person in the world.

The Smith family, consisting of mother Charlotte and her three children, Gladys, Lottie, and Jack, found themselves in a serious, almost destitute condition following the accidental death of the father. With no social safety nets like we have today, the family was forced to work for their very existence. While still a youngster, Gladys had her acting talents discovered in a variety of church and community plays. Eventually, these talents began to earn the family a few dollars when Gladys was hired on by such local talent agencies as the Cummings and Valentine stock companies. Her first substantial role was in the melodrama *The Silver King*, which was presented at the old Princess Theatre on King Street West (demolished in the early 1930s for the extension of University Avenue). Gladys was just six.

After that the youngster appeared in numerous plays before eventually being introduced to American producer David Belasco. It was at about this time (Mary's biography states that she was thirteen) that the young actress dropped her name in favour of Mary Pickford, selecting Mary as a variation of her middle name, Marie (although her birth record records that name as Louise, a name she apparently didn't like, replacing it herself with Marie) and Pickford as her maternal grandfather, John Hennessey's, middle name.

As Mary Pickford, this daughter of Toronto had a remarkable career as a silent movie star and business mogul, becoming a co-founder of United Artists.

"Our Mary" died in 1979 at the age of eighty-six, or was she eighty-seven?

April 7, 2002

Charred Ruins in Our City

One of the neat things about writing this column is the opportunity it affords me to correspond with people who have a personal connection with the Toronto of yesterday. Take Jim Croft, for instance. Some of my regular readers will be familiar with Jim's surname, as I have written about John Croft, Jim's great-grandfather, on several occasions. Unfortunately, those stories have not been happy ones, since John Croft was the only person to die as a direct result of the great fire of 1904, an inferno that destroyed much of downtown Toronto.

With next Thursday being the ninety-eighth anniversary of the outbreak of the conflagration that laid waste to more than one hundred buildings in and around the Bay and Wellington intersection, I thought I'd share with you some of the details outlined in a letter I recently received from Jim about the Croft family in Canada and in particular the unfortunate and untimely demise of his great-grandfather.

When he was only fifteen years old, John Croft, who had already spent several years working in the mines and steel mills near Sheffield, England, set off for a new life in Canada with his father, George. Immigration records indicate the pair arrived in Halifax sometime in 1881, after which they made their way westward, eventually settling in Port Hope for reasons yet to be determined. The following year George returned to England to arrange for the rest of the Croft family, which would ultimately consist of sixteen children, to join him and his third son in Ontario.

John Croft, victim of Toronto's Great Fire of 1904.

It was in Port Hope that John met and married Eliza Jane Cornish. In 1890, the young couple and their two sons moved to Toronto, where the father obtained employment as a roller maker in the factory of the Canada Printing Ink Company at the foot of Bay Street, ironically an area that would be burned several years later when the great fire of 1904 swept southward from the Bay and Wellington corner to the harbour.

Upon their arrival in Toronto, the Crofts first resided on Maple Row, a minor thoroughfare located in an area that was cleared in the early 1950s for a unique (for the time) housing project we now know as Regent Park North. Later John and the family (now consisting of two boys and a girl, two other daughters having died at the age of just five months, a sad but not unusual occurrence for the era) moved to 95 Poulette Street. It was while living here that the father started a small construction and demolition business.

We now move ahead in time to May 4, 1904, several weeks after the previously mentioned fire had swept the downtown core, leaving rows of burned-out buildings. To help get rid of the ruins that lined such main streets as Bay, Wellington, and Front, city officials put out a call for help. They desperately needed people with expertise in the use of dynamite to level what remained so that the job of getting on with rebuilding the city could begin.

John Croft, who could certainly use the money being offered for such assistance, stepped forward and was given the task of taking down the gutted Gage Building at 54–58 Front Street West (where the glittering, gold-encased Royal Bank Plaza now stands).

John carefully placed three sticks of dynamite at separate locations with the ruins, lit the fuses, and took cover. Two sticks exploded, but the third did not. Assuming it was a "dud," John re-entered the ruins

The E & S Currie Building on Wellington Street West (centre) where Toronto's Great Fire broke out on the evening of April 19, 1904.

to reset the explosive. As he inspected the unexploded stick it suddenly went off in his face. John's mangled body was quickly taken to the city's Emergency Hospital on the east side of Bay Street a few steps north of King. The young man's injuries were so severe that the family was immediately called to his bedside. Thirty-eight-year-old John Croft passed away the next day, the sole victim of Toronto's Great Fire of 1904. He was laid to rest in Mount Pleasant Cemetery.

Jim Croft's note goes on to describe how John's widow, Eliza Jane, and her three children, seventeen-year-old William, fifteen-year-old Robert, and eight-year-old Edna, carried on. With no social support as we have today, there was only William's meagre income as well as that provided by Robert, who left school that spring and became a printing pressman.

Robert married Sarah Landon in 1912 and had eight children, one of whom, Bruce, was the father of Jim, who was good enough to send me the Croft family story.

Incidentally, there are Croft streets in both Port Hope (where George and John first lived after their arrival in Canada) as well as here in Toronto. Ours was originally named Ulster, but was changed to Croft in 1908. I'd like to think it was to honour poor John. Anyone know for sure?

April 14, 2002

Glory for Leafs

Well, here we are into the Stanley Cup playoffs once again. Will this be the year for our Leafs? I'll bet more than half the present population doesn't remember the last time our guys won that (blankety-blank) trophy back on May 2, 1967. If you're among that number, let me put that ancient time into some sort of perspective.

When our Leafs last won the venerated Stanley Cup, our city was still part of the Municipality of Metropolitan Toronto, whose chairman was Bill Allen (W.R. Allen Road). In 1967, Metro's population was just under 2 million, and William Dennison was serving as Toronto's mayor. Other Metro mayors were Jack Mould (York), Ed Horton (Etobicoke), True Davidson (East York), James Service (North York), and Ab Campbell (Scarborough). In 1967 Toronto had no CN Tower, no Eaton Centre, no Blue Jays, no Skydome. The Yonge subway line ended at Eglinton station, while the Bloor-Danforth line only ran between Keele and Woodbine. The opening of the Spadina subway was still more than a decade in the future.

Even back then, a TTC fare hike was a touchy subject. People went nuts when, on March 25, 1967, a single adult fare jumped a whopping 25 percent from twenty cents to a quarter. However, you could still buy five tickets (or tokens) for a buck. Added to the cost of getting to and from the Gardens on Carlton Street, fans also had to purchase hockey tickets. In 1967, the price of regular season games

My hero, Toronto Maple Leafs player Tod Sloan.

ranged from a dollar for greys (as far up as you could go) to six dollars for boxes and rail seats.

A few of the heroes on that 1967 Stanley Cup championship team in the original six-team league included captain George Armstrong, Johnny Bower, Tim Horton, and Dave Keon (who's now helping his sister sell VIA train tickets). The Leafs defeated Montreal four games to two to win the Cup.

Actually, the first Leafs Stanley Cup victory I can recall (sort of) was the one in 1951. I was just ten, but a Leafs fan nevertheless. Of course I had the requisite woolen blue and white socks and a very itchy Leafs woolen sweater, both necessary apparel while listening to Leafs games on the radio.

Back then every Canadian kid had (as they probably still do) a favourite player. For reasons now lost in the mists of time my hero was a Leafs centre named Tod Sloan who had joined the team as a rookie in 1947. While I obviously didn't know Sloan personally, I did know his sweater number. It was eleven, and it was my number too. I had my mother stitch it on the back of my sweater while I personally applied the number in white tape (that I found in the bathroom medicine cabinet) to my skates. Maybe that's one of the reasons I was a Sloan fan. His number, eleven, was easy to assemble out of tape. But even when he changed to the more difficult number fifteen, my veneration never wavered. It took a while, but I too became number fifteen.

Interestingly, while long-time hockey fans can tell you it was defenceman Bill Barilko who scored the winning goal at two minutes

Leafs defencemen Bill Juzda (left) and Bill Barilko check out the sports pages after a game. Just a few months after scoring the winning playoff goal on this day fifty-one years ago, Barilko disappeared during a fishing trip in Northern Ontario. His remains were found in 1962.

and fifty-three seconds overtime to give the Leafs a three to two game win and a four games to one Stanley Cup victory over Montreal on this very day in 1951, I doubt if many can tell you who scored the Leafs' other two goals that game. Yup, it was my hero, Tod Sloan. I wonder where Tod is today. I'd sure like to thank him in person.

April 21, 2002

Swimming Into History

I have never used my column as a personal soapbox. However, permit me this one important exception.

Many readers will recall with great fondness the exploits of a sixteen-year-old Toronto-born schoolgirl whose unexpected triumph over Lake Ontario back in September of 1954 turned the entire nation on its ear. Loretta College student Marilyn Bell was an unwelcomed participant in a CNE-sponsored cross-lake solo swim that would have seen American distance swimmer Florence Chadwick paid $10,000 if she was able to complete the gruelling thirty-two-mile challenge, and nothing if she was unsuccessful.

Chadwick was full of confidence as she entered the water not far from the pretty little community of Youngstown, New York, her goggle-covered eyes set firmly on the finish line miles away at the CNE waterfront.

Without question, it would be a tough ordeal, one of the toughest the American had ever faced; however, just about everyone was convinced Florence could do it. In just a few hours she would become the first person to swim Lake Ontario. As for the CNE management, $10,000 was little enough to pay for all the exposure the Exhibition was to get. In addition, that chunk of prize money would be quickly replaced by the thousands who would pay the fifty-cent admission (a dime for kids) to witness Florence's historic arrival at the Ex's waterfront.

Well, as they say, the best laid plans ...

About seven hours into the swim, Chadwick was suddenly forced out, complaining of nausea and cramps. The highly touted swim was over — or was it? There in the distance, well behind where Chadwick's handlers were busy hauling the very sick American swimmer from the lake, young Marilyn Bell was being encouraged to continue by her coach, Gus Ryder. Actually, Marilyn's appearance in the lake was a surprise to many. There was nothing in it for her except the chance to better the American and to conquer the lake, as she said, "for Canada" and for the kids at the Lakeshore Swimming Club.

For more than twenty hours, the youngster fought against the lake. In fact, in the later stages of the swim that fight was carried on with Marilyn virtually unconscious. Then, at precisely 8:04 on the evening of September 9, the exhausted youngster finally touched the breakwall in front of the Boulevard Club, a spot not exactly where the CNE had hoped.

Nevertheless, Marilyn Bell had done it: she had become the first person to swim Lake Ontario. And she had actually covered forty miles, not the anticipated thirty-two.

As it would turn out, the CNE was shamed into giving the prize money to Marilyn, and to it was added a huge list of gifts she began to receive from Canadians from coast to coast. Her hometown awarded both Marilyn, and her coach, Gus Ryder, the first of the newly established Civic Awards of Merit.

Marilyn and her coach, Gus Ryder, meet Roy Rogers and Dale Evans at the 1954 CNE.

Unfortunately (and for reasons — to use a nautical term — tough to fathom) the nation has yet to recognize Marilyn with its Order of Canada (which was established in 1967, Canada's Centennial Year). Neither has the province with its own Order of Ontario, an honour initiated in 1986.

But this latter oversight may change. Initially, the Order of Ontario was awarded only to residents of Ontario. Recently, that requirement has been revised to permit residents or "former long term" residents (which Marilyn certainly had been before moving to the States in the late 1950s to be with her new husband, Joe) to receive the prestigious award.

It is now entirely appropriate to nominate our Marilyn for the Order of Ontario. Readers with internet access can find out more about the process by contacting www.gov.on.ca/citizenship/english/citdiv/honours/order.htm

Letters, faxes, and e-mails supporting her nomination and induction would also be helpful. Take a minute to tell the government how you feel about Marilyn and what she did for our city, province, and country back in 1954, and again in 1955 and 1956 when she swam the English Channel and the Strait of Juan de Fuca, respectively.

Letters should be addressed to Ontario Honours and Awards, 400 University Avenue, 2nd floor, Toronto, ON M7A 2R9; faxes to 416-314-7743; emails to nanda.casuccibyrne@mczcr@gov.on.ca.

Please note that there is some urgency as the Nominating Deadline is May 8, 2002. And thanks.

* Note: In 2003 the province finally did award Marilyn the Order of Ontario. No word yet from Order of Canada officials.

Oft times (now there's an expression you'd only see in a history column) some of the most interesting books detailing the history of a community are both written and published (usually with little or no fanfare) by an individual (or individuals) living in that community. A case in point is a new book by Ron Fletcher titled *Over the Don*. In his book, the author documents 27 vignettes of life as seen through the eyes of people who lived near the Don, crossed its various bridges or who had stepped, fallen or had been pushed into this historic river. Some of the early citizens that readers will find in this entertaining new addition to any Toronto history buff's library include Alexander Muir whose famous maple tree can be found near the corner of Queen and Leslie streets, Corneillia DeGrassi (of the DeGrassi Street family), the Reverends Green and Wood who brought religion to the communities over the Don and are remembered today in the popular Woodgreen Centre and church. A particularly interesting feature of the book, in addition to the many old photos, are the sidebar fast facts including one set that describes the origins of the names of some of the area's streets (Hunter, Hamilton, Booth, Allan, all municipal alderman). The book is available for $20 from the Riverdale Historical Society. Call 416-461-9695 for details.

April 28, 2002

Dickens of a Traveller

One of my favourite TV shows was something called *Rocky and His Friends*. And one of my favourite segments on that show was when a time-travelling dog named Peabody and his young friend, Sherman, would get into the incredible "Wayback Machine" and be transported back in time to some major historical event. Now if Peabody had ever asked me to join him in that infernal machine and set the dials to any time of my choosing, I might have suggested we return to this very day exactly 160 years ago. Arriving in Toronto on May 4, 1842, I would have set about town searching out a visitor who had stopped by while travelling from Niagara Falls to Kingston.

That person was none other than Charles Dickens, who was in the midst of a five-month-long tour of the North American continent. At thirty years of age, Dickens was already a well-known and extremely popular author whose *Pickwick Papers*, *Oliver Twist*, and *The Old Curiosity Shop* had made him famous on both sides of the Atlantic.

Dickens, who was accompanied by his wife, Katherine, had been wined and dined in Boston, New York, and Washington. As much as he appreciated the hospitality he had received from his American fans, he really had his heart set on viewing one of the wonders of the new world, the falls at Niagara. Arriving by train in Buffalo, he hastened to the Falls, describing his visit in these words: "Oh, how the

Charles Dickens as he would have looked during his visit to Toronto 160 years ago.

strife and trouble of daily life receded from my view and lessened in the distance during the ten memorable days we passed on that Enchanted Ground."

The itinerary next included a trip across the border into British North America, where Dickens was much less conspicuous, a fact much appreciated since he had been mobbed wherever he appeared in the United States.

Boarding the steamer *Transit* at the Queenston wharf, Dickens embarked on his first and only visit to Toronto. Arriving at 6:30 in the evening of May 4, 1842, the couple stayed the next two nights in the North American Hotel at the northeast corner of Yonge and Front streets. Dickens described the young city of some fifteen thousand souls thus:

> The country round this town [it had actually become a city eight years earlier] being very flat, is bare of scenic interest; but the town itself is full of life and motion, bustle, business and improvement. The streets are well paved and lighted with gas [the first lamps having been installed by a private company in December of the previous year], the houses large and good; the shops excellent. Many of them have a display of goods in their windows such as may be seen in thriving county towns in England and there are some which would do no discredit to the metropolis itself. There is a good stone prison [on the waterfront near the foot of Parliament Street] and there are besides a handsome church [the first St. James' Cathedral, which was destroyed by fire in 1849], a court house [northwest corner of King and Church], public offices, many commodious private residences and

a government observatory for noting and recording the magnetic variations [located on what is now King's College Road]. In the College of Upper Canada [northwest corner of King and Simcoe] ... a sound education ... can be had at a very moderate expense. The first stone of a new college hall [King's College, renamed the University of Toronto in 1850] had been laid but a few days before [on the site of the present Parliament Buildings]. It will be a handsome, spacious edifice, approached by a long avenue [now University Avenue which is already planted and made available as a public walk].

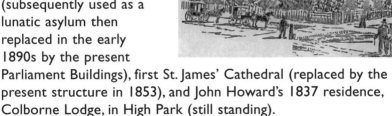

A few of the buildings Dickens would have seen during his visit (clockwise from top): King's College (subsequently used as a lunatic asylum then replaced in the early 1890s by the present Parliament Buildings), first St. James' Cathedral (replaced by the present structure in 1853), and John Howard's 1837 residence, Colborne Lodge, in High Park (still standing).

Dickens's stay was actually quite short, and he left for Kingston, then the capital of the United Canadas, on May 6.

He returned to Great Britain the following month.

Readers may be interested to know that there is an organization right here in Toronto that is devoted to the study of Dickens's many works. The Dickens Fellowship was established in Toronto in 1905 and has met continuously once a month ever since. Its charity of record is the Bloorview Hospital, thereby continuing Dickens's tradition of supporting the Great Ormand Children's Hospital in London, England. For further details on the Fellowship call 416-759-0187.

May 5, 2002

On the Trams

Once again the harried transit rider has dodged the strike bullet and there's peace once again on the TTC's 692 subway and 28 SRT cars, 1480 buses, and 248 streetcars. Since the inception of public transit in our city in 1849, there has been a total of ten disruptions to the service, ranging from a few hours to the twenty-three-day occurrence of 1974.

In addition, there have been several times when it looked as if shank's mare would be the popular way to get around town. And while money, or lack of it, was the usual reason for the disagreement, in 1938 it was something else that nearly saw the system shut down.

No, that time it all had to do with the new style of streetcar the TTC had agreed to purchase. Known as the Presidents' Conference Committee (PCC) Streamliner, this revolutionary vehicle was the "state of the art" sixty-four years ago. It had been created with input from a variety of transit operators in the United States and Canada, including staff of the TTC, resulting in a vehicle that had operating characteristics far superior to anything then in operation on city streets.

The new PCCs had several advantages over the TTC's older equipment. They were faster (automobile drivers were warned not to try to cut in front when racing away from a green traffic light), could stop quicker (this time drivers were warned not to sit too close behind the new cars), had smoother acceleration (fewer passengers cascaded into other passengers when the new cars left a stop), were warmer in the

A REQUEST FOR TRAFFIC CO-OPERATION

New Street Cars in Regular Service, Saturday Sept. 24th

NEXT SATURDAY the new T.T.C. street cars will be placed in regular service.

The new street cars have much more rapid pick-up than the street cars to which other traffic in Toronto has been accustomed. Moreover, the new cars gather speed quietly and smoothly.

The braking systems enable the new street cars to reduce speed and to stop much more quickly.

The Operators of the new cars will, of course, make all possible allowance for other traffic not yet accustomed to the pace of the new T.T.C. cars.

It is recommended that drivers of other vehicles keep these points in mind:

CROSSING AND TURNING—Drivers of other vehicles should allow themselves more time and space than formerly before turning or crossing in front of the new street cars. "Cutting in" is, of course, undesirable at any time.

FOLLOWING AND STOPPING—The new street cars can vary their pace and can stop much more quickly than the street cars Toronto has had. It is advisable that drivers of other vehicles bear this in mind when following or stopping behind the new street cars.

TURNING OUT FROM CURB—Vehicles turning out from the curb should not turn into the path of an approaching street car.

The Commission requests the co-operation of all users of the streets, so that the period required for introducing the new street cars may be as short and as free from accidents as possible.

TORONTO TRANSPORTATION COMMISSION

Above: TTC crews off-load one of the first PCC cars to arrive in the city, 1938.

Left: Newspaper announcements warn automobile drivers to be wary of the modern new PCC model streetcars.

winter, would decrease the headways between cars, and each came equipped with nice, comfortable upholstered and padded seats.

Unfortunately, the new cars did have one problem, something that the TTC either didn't see coming or perhaps hoped would simply go away on its own. And what was the problem? The PCC car was intended to be operated by only one man. While the Commission had operated a few one-man cars since its inception in 1921, the majority of the fleet was of the two-man (operator and conductor) variety. And while the introduction of the PCC cars on the St. Clair route in October had gone smoothly, as more and more of the new cars arrived motormen and conductors began refusing to sign up for the Bloor and Dundas routes, the next to have the new one-man cars.

They felt that an obvious result of the purchase of 140 one-man cars would be extensive layoffs. (By the way, I did not create the terms "one-man cars" and "two-man cars." Back then that's exactly what they were. Women had yet to be hired as operators. It would take a world war to change that fact.)

All throughout early November 1938, the city's streetcar riders were bombarded with stories issued by both the TTC and the Union. Would there be a strike, or would the cars keep running? For a time it looked grim.

Eventually, however, the two sides agreed on a plan that would see the establishment of a guaranteed six-day, thirty-six-hour week for the majority of operators, with guarantees that the senior motormen and conductors would be kept on the two-man cars that operated as "Extras" during rush hours.

Transit calm quickly returned to the system, and before long the new one-man cars began appearing on routes all over town. But never on Yonge.

Legacy Sportswear has recently introduced a new line of casual clothing, mugs, key chains, etc. that feature the TTC's legendary PCC streetcar. The full "TTC Stuff" catalogue can be perused at www.legacysportswear.com. Information on where the items can be purchased is available by calling 905-856-5289.

May 12, 2002

Thirty-Five Years on the Go

It was exactly thirty-five years ago this coming Thursday that GO Transit, described in newspaper reports of May 23, 1967, as "the nation's first specially designed rail commuter service," began operations. The first service provided by the new GO project on that day was along the sixty-mile Lakeshore route between Hamilton on the west and Pickering on the east. Officiating was the provincial premier of the day, John Robarts, accompanied by his Highways Minister George Gomme and CNR vice-president D.V. Gonder. The first eastbound train left the Oakville station at 5:50 A.M., the first westbound from Pickering at 6:00 A.M.

Interestingly, the concept of a transportation system that would provide access to and from Toronto for people living outside its borders had been pioneered almost a century earlier. These lines began as privately financed routes using high-speed electric trains serving communities such as Port Credit, Georgetown, and Guelph to the west, and Woodbridge, Richmond Hill, Newmarket ,and even Sutton to the north.

And while plans had been initiated to connect Toronto with communities east of the city (Oshawa, Port Perry, Lindsay, and Peterborough), and in a few cases the physical rights-of-way had even been purchased, these eastern routes never materialized.

Collectively, the lines were known as "radials," a term penned by Sir Adam Beck, creator and first chairman of Ontario Hydro. The word was descriptive of the way the lines radiated out from Toronto.

Radial car on the Toronto–Richmond Hill route, *circa* 1915.

Artist's concept of GO Transit's proposed new downtown Toronto bus terminal.

While politics were to eventually doom Beck's radials, there's little doubt that the main culprit was proliferation of cars and trucks. These vehicles prompted the construction of miles of new highways. Government money was tight, and soon the radials were being ignored. Beck's dream eventually died.

As the years passed, an ever-increasing number of cars and trucks began to overwhelm much of the province's highway system. The subject of an inter-city rail commuter system again became a popular topic. For a time, both the CNR and CPR got into the commuter rail business, eventually "pooling" their services. However, the fact that there was more money in carrying freight than there was in carrying people put an end to that idea. Now the pressure was on the provincial government to do something.

The birth of the present GO Transit operation can be traced back to 1963 when the province initiated a study to determine what existing facilities might be acceptable for use as commuter train corridors. That study revealed that of the 280 miles of track throughout the metropolitan Toronto region, approximately 90 percent, or 250 miles, could be adapted to commuter train use that would involve one or two trains daily in each direction. Of that figure, eighty or so miles were located between the communities of Burlington and Pickering and centred on Toronto.

Two years later, a survey was conducted among the people living in the Burlington-Pickering corridor to see if they would use a commuter service if one were to be established. The results of that survey revealed that approximately ninety thousand people drove their cars in an east-west direction when going to work each day.

Of that number nearly half were headed into Toronto.

Surveying this latter group, nearly fifteen thousand said they would use a commuter train service if one were available. That was good enough for the government, and on May 17, 1965, Premier Robarts announced the creation of a rail commuter service for the Toronto area. It was to be a three-year experiment. And in spite of an American transit expert's prediction GO would be a failure, by the end of its first full year in business GO had carried more than 4 million commuters (an average of 15,363 each working day) on its single Lakeshore route.

(By comparison, GO Transit presently serves 165,000 commuters each working day and last year carried a total of 43 million passengers.)

To supplement its train service, GO Transit began introducing bus routes. In 1989 a few of those buses began loading and unloading near the busy Front and Bay Street intersection. Now, approximately two hundred use the on-street terminal each workday. The congestion and resulting impact on schedules soon became intolerable.

There was no doubt that a new bus terminal to serve Union Station was an absolute necessity.

Not that the idea of such a terminal was new. In fact, the billion-dollar Metro Centre project of the early 1970s (that would have seen the demolition of most of Union Station) had made provisions for a new bus terminal. When that project died, so too did the new terminal. Things got so bad that in 1977 a Toronto newspaper ran an editorial pointing out the obvious, "Toronto Needs a New Bus Terminal." Again, nothing happened.

Finally, late last month ground was broken for a new $3.1-million GO Transit bus terminal to be located between Yonge and Bay streets just south of the Federal Building. Buses will begin to use this new facility in July.

May 19, 2002

"Best Used Car Buy in Town"

For many years during the 1950s and '60s, one of the most popular advertising jingles on radio went like this:

Buying or selling a car?
Try Ted Davy, Ted Davy, Ted Davy,
Just one location 901 on Danforth Avenue,
For the best used car buy in the town,
Try Ted Davy, Ted Davy, Ted Davy.

Born in the Parkdale area of Toronto in 1915, Ted Davy's first job once he left school was to book bands into some of the many dance halls and clubs scattered all across the city.

But selling cars was in Ted's blood, and he eventually obtained full-time employment with the A.D. Gorries dealership on Gerrard Street East. In 1941, he opened his own used car lot on Queen Street East. Within a few years, Ted had closed this lot and moved to the Danforth, the city's used car district, where he opened a pair of lots at #901 (opposite Donlands Avenue) and #1301 at the corner of Lamb — later the site of another well-known used car dealer on the Danforth, Kenny Kars.

However, within a few short years Ted decided to put all his efforts into a single property, which was destined over time to become a true city landmark. It was at 901 Danforth Avenue that the Ted Davy organization sold as many as ten thousand used cars annually. Interestingly, this figure was frequently questioned by used car dealers from south of the border who just couldn't believe that ten thousand used cars could be sold from just one location in a single twelve-month period.

Ted retired from the used car business in the early 1980s and eventually moved to Keswick, Ontario, in 1987. Here he and his son Doug (who assisted me with the details found in this article) established a housing development at what is called Davy Point.

Ted Davy passed away at the Newmarket Hospital on March 18 at the age of eighty-seven. A special memorial service in honour of Ted's full and interesting life will be held at 11:00 a.m., May 28, at Islington United Church, 25 Burnamthorpe Road, Etobicoke, ON. All Ted's friends are welcome.

The always busy Ted Davy checks out one of his hundreds of used cars prior to another sale, *circa* **1955.**

One of the most popular attractions ever held at the annual Canadian National Exhibition was the Scottish World Festival Tattoo. The idea of holding this type of attraction to salute Canadian Scots and the Scottish heritage in Canada was initiated in 1970 when the suggestion was made that the world bagpiping championship be held during the running of the CNE.

When it was discovered that Scotland had no intention of giving up the event, the CNE's then general manager David Garrick came up with the idea that a giant tattoo be held instead. And he had just the right man on staff to produce it: Lieutenant Colonel Cliff Hunt, who had headed up numerous similar events during his long tenure as the chief of music for the Canadian Armed Forces.

The first Scottish World Festival Tattoo was held during the 1972 Exhibition. To kick off that year's fair a spectacular parade consisting of twenty-five hundred pipers and drummers marched their way from the provincial Parliament Buildings along Wellesley Street, down Yonge and across Queen to the seven-year-old "new" City Hall, where Mayor William Denisson took the salute. Police estimated that the parade was seen by nearly a quarter-million people.

Unfortunately, as popular as the Scottish World Festival was, drawing hundreds of thousands from all over Eastern Canada and the United States to Toronto and the CNE's gigantic Grandstand, the costs to present the Scottish World Festival Tattoo became prohibitive. The last one was held in 1981.

Some of the many participants in the second edition of the festival, which was held in 1973, parade in front of the now demolished CNE Grandstand. Note that the singers and dancers with the Soviet Red Army were another feature attraction that year.

While the CNE's tattoo died more than twenty years ago, the Hamilton International Tattoo lives on just a short drive down the Queen Elizabeth Highway. This year's event will next take place on the evening of June 8 and again in the afternoon of June 9 at Copp's Coliseum in downtown Hamilton. Featured performers will be the Royal Hamilton Light Infantry and the famous Argyll and Sutherland Highlanders of Canada, whose origins go back nearly a century. Guest participants in the show will include the USAF Honor Guard Drill team from Washington, D.C., and the West Point Military Academy's "Hellcats."

Information on ticket prices, event times and other participants is available on-line (www.hamiltontattoo.ca).

May 26, 2002

Charting Toronto Harbour

A couple of Sundays ago I spent a very cold afternoon on the edge of Toronto Bay at Harbourfront Centre. How cold was it, that spring afternoon? Well, the last time I was that cold I had just fallen into a pool of slush and my breeks with the leather knee patches had frozen to my very young skin.

Fortunately some nice person in the Arctic Canada store at Queen's Quay Terminal (which interestingly is owned and operated by the country's newest territory, Nunavut) eventually came out and draped David Brightling and myself in a couple of warm Arctic blankets. David is the former general manager of the Royal Canadian Yacht Club, and you'd be hard-pressed to find a more knowledgeable person on "Sharks," "Dragonflies," and dinghies than David. Together we provided nearly four hours of commentary as several hundred boats and ships sailed past the commodores' reviewing stand and those members of the public that were hardy enough to face the chill weather. I half expected to see iceboats in the sailpast.

The event was held to commemorate the 150th anniversary of the establishment of the RCYC in 1852. The vessels in this sailpast (said to be the largest ever seen on Toronto Bay) represented the three yacht clubs on Toronto Island: the Island Yacht Club (established in 1951), the Queen City Yacht Club (1889), and, of course, the RCYC.

Just a few of the many changes in and around Toronto's waterfront are evident in these contrasting photos taken nearly a half-century apart looking north from the foot of York Street.

In addition, the sailpast featured *Empire Sandy* (built in 1943), *Kajama* (1930), and *Oriole 9* (1987), just a few of the many charter boats seen on the bay. Interestingly, Toronto now has the largest number of tour boats of any port on the continent.

Also making appearances were the Toronto-to-Niagara hydrofoil *Seaflight 1* (built in 1996 and originally a Caribbean fast ferry), the

Toronto Port Authority's tug *William Rest* (1961 and named in honour of Bill Rest, who joined the Toronto Harbour Commission in 1915), and the Toronto fireboat *William Lyon Mackenzie* (in service since 1964 and named for Toronto's first mayor).

Coincident with this historic harbour event was the publication of a new book on the history of Toronto Harbour by my long-time friend Ted Wickson. I first met Ted when he worked for the TTC many years ago. Several years ago we worked on a book titled *The TTC Story, the First 75 Years* (still available from the Sun News Research Centre).

Some time ago Ted began compiling photos and writing text for a comprehensive new book on the fascinating history of the Toronto's harbour. The book covers such diverse topics as early trading days at York (as Toronto was called prior to 1834), the railways and harbour trust, the creation of the Port Industrial District, building the railway viaduct, the arrival of the airplane on Toronto's waterfront, recreation and aquatic sports on the bay, memories of Sunnyside Amusement Park, and milestones in the harbour's long history.

Reflections of Toronto Harbour, 200 Years of Port Activity and Waterfront Development is a 178-page hardcover book with more than 200 photos (many in colour), maps, and a glossary, and it is available from the Toronto Port Authority for $75 (plus tax and postage). Call 416-863-2000 for ordering details.

June 2, 2002

Life's a Beach

I'm often asked if I ever run out of story ideas for this column. The quick and simple answer is no. Even though I've been contributing articles to the *Sunday Sun* for more than a quarter of a century, our community's history is so rich that I'm pretty sure there are enough stories for many years to come, God and Quebecer willing.

In addition to the items that come to me through the perusal of old newspapers and books, there are those that come my way right "out of the blue" from readers and friends who know of my interests.

The large picture in this week's column is an example of the latter. It is one of several that arrived in the mail from Rick Schofield, who I'm convinced knows Scarborough's history better than anyone I have ever met. The letter that accompanied Rick's offering simply suggested I might like these photos for my collection, no doubt because they featured some streetcars, though of the drowned variety.

In fact what we see in this aerial photo are some ex-TTC Peter Witt streetcars beached on shoals somewhere along the northern reaches of the Humber River. As the TTC acquired the more modern PCC Streamliner type of streetcar (either new or used from such cities as Birmingham, Alabama, and Cincinnati, Ohio, who deemed the electric streetcar obsolete and converted to bus operation) many of its old Witt streetcars were considered surplus. This number increased dramatically with the opening of the Yonge subway in late March 1954.

Ex-TTC streetcars somewhere on the Humber River, October 1954.

This is the type of streetcar seen in the photograph above; it is seen westbound on St. Clair Avenue just west of Spadina, *circa* 1948. This particular car, #2646, was a Brill Witt built in 1922 and was one of many similar cars eventually sold for scrap in 1953–54.

The vast majority of these old cars were simply sold for a few dollars to scrap metal dealers. Some, however, were acquired by individuals who converted them into dwellings. My guess is that the cars in this photo were part of a trailer camp somewhere on the upper Humber, and when the river flooded during the unwelcomed arrival of Hurricane Hazel on October 15, 1954, they were simply swept away in the torrent.

Are there any readers who can expand on this story? Drop me a line c/o the *Sunday Sun*, 333 King Street East, Toronto, ON, M5A 3X5.

June 9, 2002

Have a Right Royal Visit

One of Toronto's true landmarks is the good old King Edward Hotel, which has just entered its one hundredth year in the hospitality business. That's not to say that prior to the arrival of the new hotel in 1903 the city was void of hotels. Far from it. In fact, the city directory issued the year before the "King Eddy" opened listed a grand total of 183 places to stay in a city that boasted a population of just over 200,000 citizens.

Most of those listed in the directory were formerly old houses that had had their large rooms divided into small rooms, beds and closets added, and a catchy name painted on a sign out front announcing to the weary traveller that this was the Albion Hotel (33–35 Jarvis Street, operated by J. Mossop, who years later opened a new place on Yonge Street that, nicely renovated, is now known as the Hotel Victoria), the Caledonia House (Queen and York), the Whynot Hotel (248 Queen Street West — I can hear it now: "Shall we find a hotel?" said the young man to his girlfriend. "Whynot," she replied.), the British Lion (62 Queen Street West), or the Rising Sun Hotel (666 Yonge Street). While on the subject of the Sun, one of community's earliest hotels, Jordan's York Hotel, stood right where the Toronto Sun Building is located today at 333 King Street East.

In most of these hotels, rooms were available by the day, week, month, or year. In fact, some city hotels were used by many Torontonians as their permanent residence.

King Edward Hotel, King St. East, Toronto, Can.

Left: The new King Edward Hotel was a favourite subject for souvenir postcards. Note that the east tower has yet to be constructed in this *circa* 1910 view looking east along King.

Below: The King of King Edward. He reigned from 1903 to 1910.

Without doubt the best known of the "pre-King Eddy" hotels was the Queen's. It stood on Front Street opposite today's Union Station, on a site now occupied by Toronto's best-known hostelry, the Fairmont Royal York. While the Queen's was the place to stay in late-nineteenth-century Toronto (both by reputation and proximity to the railway station), it had actually started out as a row of houses that were converted into a school. This school was subsequently turned into a hotel that was known as first as Sword's then as the Revere House. In 1862, under a new owner, entrepreneur and steamboat captain Thomas Dick, the swankier name Queen's was chosen.

For the next several decades the Queen's, the Walker House (York and Front) and to a lesser extent the Rossin House (later known as the Prince George, at King and York), the Shakespeare Hotel (later the Imperial, also at the King and York intersection), the Winchester Hotel (Parliament and Winchester), and the Elliott House (Shuter and Church, burned in a tragic fire, then a parking lot for years and soon the site of a new condo tower) were the major hotels in town.

With this eclectic mix of hotels scattered across the city it's no wonder that Torontonians were in awe when businessman and banker George Gooderham announced in 1898, on behalf of a new enterprise he had founded, the Toronto Hotel Company, that work would soon start on a palatial new hotel for Toronto. It would be named, now that all the necessary approvals had been received from London, in honour of the reigning monarch. The hotel would be located on the south side of King Street (a thoroughfare named after a different king, in this instance King George III) just east of Yonge in the heart of the city. Actually, the new hotel's location east of Yonge Street was a bit surprising, considering that the city's business district was moving west of Yonge. Gooderham's business interests east of the main street made the site selection obvious.

The public's collective jaws dropped even further when the King Edward Hotel began to take shape. It was to be a stunning structure. Toronto architect Edward James Lennox, who had recently designed the city's glorious Municipal Building and Court House on Queen Street West at the top of Bay and who would soon begin work on Sir Henry Pellatt's new house on the hill, Casa Loma (a direct translation), had seen to that. There was no question that the young architect had done himself proud with his newest creation.

Even while construction was going on, the company decided that the hotel would be such an obvious success that it really needed a couple more floors. Suddenly, what Lennox had designed as a six-storey structure became eight. The company's intuition was right, and from the day the new hotel opened in 1903 it was a money-maker. Not only were its rooms almost always full, but so too were its various dining and other social and business rooms. In the late teens work commenced on a sixteen-floor addition that would join the east side of the original building. Though not as majestic as the original part of the hotel, it helped make the hotel the largest in the city, at least until the new Royal York opened in June 1929.

Since then, the King Eddy's fortunes have waxed and waned (at one point it was slated for demolition), but as the "grand old man of King East" enters its centennial year all looks bright. Great party plans are being made, and as they're announced I'll keep readers informed.

June 16, 2002

Recipe for a Riot

By and large the citizens of our fair city are a law-abiding bunch. That's not to say that things have never gotten out of control. In recent years a few brainless hooligans have done damage to stores on lower Yonge Street and to the Legislative Buildings in Queen's Park (for reasons they probably now forget), while the government's so-called summit meetings often bring out the worst in people. (Why not teleconference or hold them in Nunavut?)

Many years ago the city's annual Orange Day parade would often erupt into a series of pitched battles as local Catholics and Protestants battled one another over events that had happened thousands of miles away and many centuries before. In fact, on more than one occasion the mayor of the day, being concerned that things would deteriorate to the point where they would be more than his police force could handle, called out the militia to keep an eye on things. You know, in some respects we're better today than we were in the so-called good old days. King Billy's July 12 "walks" no longer provide the flashpoint they once did. Where thousands used to participate, it's hard now to tell when the parade starts and when it ends.

Not only were religious beliefs the cause of annual "punch-ups" in our Toronto of a century ago, so too were the dictates of the city's then privately run streetcar company. Low pay, long hours, and draconian rules (such as the ones that forced the streetcar operators to stand for

Courtesy TTC Archives.

Toronto Railway Company operators and conductors of the era pose outside the old Roncesvalles car house.

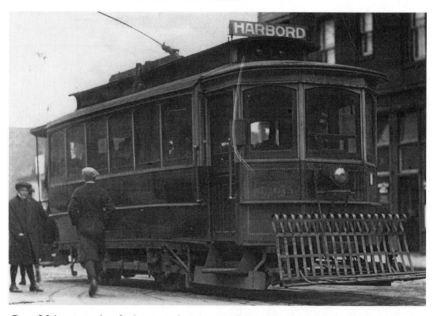

Car 306, typical of those whose windows were smashed during the streetcar riot one hundred years ago yesterday. This car was also one of the first of the all-new electric streetcars introduced in 1892. It's now on display at the National Science and Technology Museum in Ottawa.

their entire shift and to pay for broken trolley poles out of their own pockets) often led to labour strife.

One such struggle came to a violent climax exactly one hundred years ago yesterday. As mentioned, back then the city's public transportation needs were provided by the cars and men of the Toronto Railway Company (TRC). The TRC took over in 1891 after a brief attempt by the city to provide service. The company was under the control of the domineering William Mackenzie, who, with his other national railway interests, both steam and electric, was often referred to as the young country's "Railway King." (Mackenzie's story is told in great detail in Rae Fleming's noteworthy book *The Railway King of Canada* from UBC Press). Two years after Mackenzie's TRC began operations, and after much hostility, the workers unionized and, on August 24, 1893, were recognized as members of Division 113 of the Amalgamated Brotherhood of Street Railway Workers (known today as Amalgamated Transit Union, Local 113).

Things went relatively smoothly until June 21, 1902, when, having asked management for more money and having been refused, the men went out on strike. Streetcar service continued that day with the men who continued to work receiving a full day's pay. Wages amounted to fifteen cents an hour for first-year men and eighteen cents for senior staff with three years' service or more. There were no problems the first day, but when the early cars were put out on the following day, things deteriorated rapidly. Stikers, sympathizers, and just plain hoodlums stoned the cars and the car barns on King Street East and on Roncesvalles and Yorkville avenues. Every window on every car that appeared on city streets was smashed. Those who had attempted to operate the cars were yanked from their vehicles and beaten by a mob that was eventually held at bay and prevented from doing more damage (and perhaps serious injury to the men) only by the presence of mounted police.

The city's chief magistrate, Mayor Oliver Aikin Howland, was concerned that things would deteriorate even further and requested that the militia be called out. With nearly fourteen hundred members of the Governor General's Bodyguards, the Royal Grenadiers, the Toronto Mounted Rifles, the Hussars, and the Dragoons soon patrolling city streets, calmness returned city streets one hundred years ago today.

Cooler heads agreed to submit the monetary issues to an arbitrator, and the next day, the start of a new workweek, things were back on the rails. The employees were pacified, receiving an extra few cents an hour.

June 23, 2002

Lighting Up 135 Candles

Tomorrow is our nation's 135th birthday. Back then the new Dominion of Canada consisted of just four provinces: Ontario and Quebec (which up until that time had been known as Upper and Lower Canada, respectively), New Brunswick, and Nova Scotia. And while there were many reasons for the four to join in confederation, one of the chief reasons was for defence purposes. There was little doubt that the Union's defeat of the Confederacy south of the border after four long years of war did not bode well for the future of British North America. Many on this side of the border were convinced that the next move on the part of the militarily ready United States of America was an attack on Britain's colonies to the north. Confederation of the four provinces would strengthen their collective resolve to remain loyal to the monarch.

Toronto, on that first Confederation Day, had a population of nearly fifty thousand living in a community bounded by Dufferin Street to the west, Bloor to the north, the Don River to the east, and south of Queen Street to the lake as far as MacLean Avenue. Toronto Bay was the site of a busy grain and lumber business and was frequently jammed in the warmer months with sailing schooners loading and unloading cargo at wharves long since covered over as the burgeoning city pushed its southern boundary further and further into the bay. The Leafs, Raptors, Argos, and Blue Jays all now play where water once flowed.

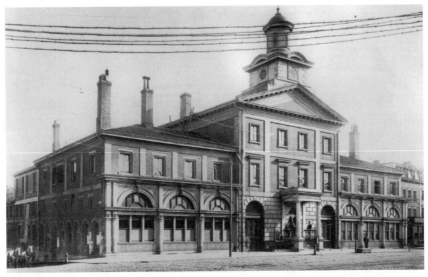

Toronto's City Hall in Confederation Year was at the southwest corner of Front and Jarvis streets. The centre portion is incorporated in the South St. Lawrence Market. The Council Chamber is now home to the Market Gallery. Both the market and its upstairs gallery are fascinating places to visit.

Along the water's edge, wood-burning railway engines chugged in and out of the thirty-three-year-old city's not one, but three, waterfront train stations. Horse-drawn streetcars (sleighs in winter) made their way along a little more than four miles of track on two of the city's main thoroughfares, Yonge and Queen, as well as on a portion of a third. The Yonge cars operated a twenty-minute service from the St. Lawrence Market west along King and north on Yonge into suburban Yorkville. The latter route went from the market via King and Yonge to Queen then west to the intersection with old

Mayor James Edward Smith (photo from the Boston Mills Press book *Mayors of Toronto* by Victor Russell, 1982).

Dundas Street, now the Queen-Ossington corner. Cash fares only were accepted, and they were set at a nickel. Most of the streets were still dirt, with the busiest routes macadamized.

Amenities taken for granted today were still pretty primitive in the Toronto of 1867. Most still drank water from the bay, while indoor plumbing was a luxury enjoyed by a very few of the citizens. Interior illumination still relied on coal oil and candles, while a couple of streets boasted gas lights installed and maintained by Consumers' Gas (a company now known as Enbridge). There were 180 hotels in the Toronto of 1867 (the Queen's on Front Street West and the Rossin House at King and York being the largest), 67 butchers, 34 pawn shops, 31 bakers, 12 plumbers, 9 dentists, and 1 chiropodist.

Another fact of life (then as now) was death, with most burials being conducted in the Anglican Cemetery of St. James on north Parliament Street and the Catholic St. Michael's Cemetery on Yonge near Deer Park (St. Clair Avenue). Others found final refuge within the non-denominational Necropolis that overlooked the meandering and burbling waters of the Don River at the end of Winchester Street. This trio of burial grounds still exist, though St. Michael's has been closed and the Don neither meanders nor burbles.

Toronto's mayor in 1867 was a chap named James Edward Smith, who was born in England and came to Toronto with his family in 1841. He enjoyed a successful business career as a wholesale grocery, wine, and liquor merchant, insurance agent, and land speculator. Smith entered municipal politics in 1857, and in 1867 he was appointed mayor by his fellow council members. (In those days elections were annual events with the voter's choice of mayor in vogue from 1859 to 1866. Then, after seven years at the whim of city council, the public's selection was resumed in 1874.)

It was Mayor Smith who oversaw the party that celebrated Canada's emergence as a country. A review of the troops took place on the Bathurst Street Common (near the fort) while later that evening up at Queen's Park (dedicated six years earlier by the Prince of Wales in honour of his mother, Victoria, the Queen) there was an "instrumental Promenade Concert" and massive fireworks display. Happy Birthday Canada!!

June 30, 2002

In the Market for a Change

Every once in a while, a windfall of material related to Toronto's history comes my way. The latest occurred one evening while I was visiting the monthly gathering of the Weston Historical Society. After the meeting a nice lady who lived in North Bay and was in Toronto visiting her sister, who was a member of the executive of the society, presented me with a selection of views of Toronto that had been printed from old negatives that were in the family's possession. My benefactor explained she didn't know anything about the images but was sure I would find them of interest.

Well, the one reproduced here is of special interest for a couple of reasons. First, it was taken at the historic St. Lawrence Market (which, if anyone in charge of that place is reading this column, will be two hundred years old next year), and second, this rare view shows the testing of what was called a fender, or lifeguard, on one the new electric streetcars while curious market-goers look on. The photo orientation is looking northwest from the building that stood at the southeast corner, where the Times Square condominium is now located. The street running left to right in the view is Front, the one to the extreme right, running north-south, is Jarvis. A corner of West Market Street (now a pedestrian walkway) shows at the top right.

Now, as to what is going on in the photo.

When the new electric streetcars were first introduced on Toronto

A close examination of this rare photo reveals a "victim" caught in the fender of this early electric streetcar as crowds look on. The building in the background is the south end of the old North St. Lawrence Market.

Courtesy of the Times Square condominium management and Mr. and Mrs. Viera.

A similar view from one of the condo balconies on the southeast corner of Jarvis and Front streets.

city streets in August 1892, many serious accidents involving pedestrians soon followed. This unfortunate fact was probably because the new cars were much faster and quieter than the horse-drawn vehicles to which they were accustomed. For more than thirty years city streets had echoed with the clip-clop sound of the street railway's slow, plodding horses.

Louis H. Pursley's marvellous book *Street Railways of Toronto, 1861–1921* records that it was in 1902 that the Toronto Railway Company first began experimenting with devices to either deflect or scoop up wayward pedestrians before they were run down. These were called Watson fenders and came in a variety of shapes and styles.

When the Peter Witt and PCC Streamliner cars were introduced they came equipped with cradles that dropped down when an object struck a bar suspended underneath the front of the car. Today's CLRV cars have no cradles, the ALRVs do.

July 7, 2002

Art at the Market Gallery

Hidden away on the second floor of the South St. Lawrence Market at the corner of Front and Jarvis streets is the Market Gallery, where, in an upstairs area that was formerly the Council Chamber in Toronto's first purpose-built city hall, the city displays its many art and archival treasures. And almost as interesting as the constantly changing exhibitions is the building itself.

The central portion of the present South Market, and the section that since 1979 has housed the Market Gallery, dates back to 1844–45 and was part of Toronto's first purpose-built city hall. I use the term "purpose-built" since there was another city hall before it, and while the story is a bit confusing, stay with me. Believe me, it's worth it.

When the former Town of York was elevated to city status on March 6, 1834, and the young community's name changed back to the pre–John Simcoe Toronto, its council members continued to meet in what had been the Town Hall. This unimpressive little structure was located where the St. Lawrence Hall stands today and by default became the city's first city hall, literally overnight.

It was in use for nearly a decade before a new city hall was completed and ready for occupation. This one, erected at the southwest corner of Front and Jarvis streets, was the first purpose-built city hall and was to remain in use for the next fifty-four years.

This remarkable photo from Larry Becker's collection now on display at Toronto's Market Gallery shows workmen putting the finishing touches on the papier maché arch that straddled the Bay and Richmond intersection in the heart of the city. It was erected in honour of the 1901 visit of the Duke and Duchess of Cornwall and York (who became King George V and Queen Mary).

Then on September 18, 1899, the building was abandoned when all the officials and bureaucrats (yup, even then) moved uptown into what we now refer to as "Old" City Hall at the top of Bay Street.

A year or so later two new buildings were built on the east and west sides of the "ancient" (well, ancient for this city) Front and Jarvis structure and a huge roof was erected over the three, thereby creating what we now call the South St. Lawrence Market.

The present exhibition at the Market Gallery (and running through to the end of September) is titled "Collecting Toronto: Through the Eyes of Larry Becker" and is based on one of the largest private donations of artifacts and archival materials ever made to the City of Toronto.

I first met Larry when he was running a small stamp and coin store on Yonge Street just north of Lawrence. Even then he had Toronto memorabilia in the form of city newspapers, rare old transportation tickets, tokens and transfers, school sports meet plaques, CNE ribbons, and the like scattered all over the place. He then moved into a large warehouse in the Downsview area where the collection mushroomed in size until that barn of a place as well as his house were both full "to the brim."

Following Larry's untimely death in 1998, the family arranged to have his treasures turned over to the city he loved. The items on display at the Market Gallery are but a fraction of his gigantic collection. Visitors will see old school report cards, the first Maple Leaf Gardens program, Fenian war medals, First World War snapshots, Edwardian postcards, tiny tickets for the city's horse-drawn streetcars, a dance card from the reception given for the young Prince of Wales during his Toronto visit in 1860, and more, so much more.

If you haven't had reason to visit the gallery up until now, and you're a fan of our city's history, please don't miss this show. Oh, and it's free. For times, call the Market Gallery at 416-392-7604 or visit www.city.toronto.on.ca/culture and follow the links.

July 14, 2002

Ahh, Those Good Old Days

How many remember the good old days when you would drive into the parking lot at the local A&W restaurant and by simply flashing the car headlights, a young lady on roller skates would quickly arrive at the car door to take your order? She'd soon be back with the food on a serving tray that would be affixed to a half-rolled-down car window. You'd eat the meal and, once finished the burger, fries, and root beer, simply flash the lights again and here she comes to take away the tray and leftovers.

You know, I think about that old A&W restaurant (now where was it, north Avenue Road or was it on Bathurst Street, can't remember for sure) every time I have my classic 1955 Pontiac out for a spin.

Something else I think about is what things were like when my car, a turquoise and white Laurentian hardtop, rolled off the assembly line out at GM's Oshawa car plant.

Hey, now here's a coincidence: that happened on this very day in 1955. And here's a copy of the *Toronto Telegram* newspaper for that day. That'll be five cents a copy, please.

Let's see, now. What were the main stories on July 21, 1955, the day my classic was "born"?

Toronto was in the midst of a heat wave, 93 degrees today, 95 tomorrow (note that the temperature is only in Fahrenheit). The TTC had been facing a fare hike, but money from Metro Toronto would

With only twenty-one hundred of my model built, what are the chances that this 1955 Pontiac Laurentian sitting in front of Trull's on the Danforth near Greenwood in this photo is mine?

allow the adult cash fare to remain at fifteen cents cash and another dime for travel out into the suburban "Zones." (That was when passengers paid for the distance travelled on the TTC. Will we see that again as a way to help the cash-strapped Commission?) Metro Chairman Fred Gardiner was also assuring residents of North York that there would be an adequate supply of water for the rest of the summer, meaning that lawn watering could continue.

Mayor Nathan Phillips was encouraging Torontonians to "get serious" and learn what to do in the event of an H-Bomb raid on the city. He praised the Tely for building a demonstration H-Bomb shelter at City Hall (now "Old" City Hall) so that citizens could see what they should be looking at building.

An editorial in that day's paper urged that the building of the Burlington Skyway bridge be speeded up. Another agreed with the recent decision to turn Malton (now Pearson International) Airport over to the federal government. Now work could start on a much-needed $22-million expansion of the city's outdated airport. (Will it ever end? A $4.4-billion program is presently underway.)

Seat belts were few and far between in 1955. In 1964, good old Canadian Tire was selling them as well as safety running lights, something all new cars have today.

Down at the CNE grounds, General Motors was presenting its "Parade of Progress" under the "Giant Silver Aerodrome." Visitors to the show could see first-hand "food cooked on a cold stove" (microwave), "a motor that runs on sunshine" (solar power), and a batch of "synthetic rubber, made right before your eyes." Oh, there were "jets and rockets" as well.

On July 21, 1955, Loblaw's was advertising side bacon at sixty-nine cents a pound (per kilogram wasn't even mentioned), Kraft dinners were fifteen cents each, a quart of regular milk (no litres) was twenty cents, and a dozen large eggs were fifty-four cents. Twenty-five of their Toronto area stores were listed as being "air conditioned."

Need a place to cook and eat that food? A four-bedroom house was advertised for sale in the quiet Moore Park part of town for $19,500. Or, if that was too much money to spend, a new five-room bungalow at 269 Erskine Avenue in North Toronto was available for only $16,800.

Rather than cooking, why not go out for dinner? The same paper ran a plateful of ads for restaurants that today are only memories. Remember these: the Town Tavern on Queen East at Yonge, Dell Tavern, Cottage Restaurant, Sign of the Steer, Ciccone's, Waller's, Steele's, and Letros? A couple , the Town and Country and Lindy's, are still in business.

With television still very much in its infancy in the 1950s (Toronto had but a single station, CBLT, which was still to be found on Channel 9) people relied a great deal on their local movie house to get away from things. On the day my Pontiac rolled off the line these were just a few of the films being shown around town: *Dam Busters* at the University and

Eglinton, *It Came From Beneath the Sea* at the Glendale, State, and Downtown, *Interrupted Melody* at the Loew's, *Kind Hearts and Coronets* plus *The Man in the White Suit* at the Hyland and Christie, *Man Without a Star* at the Midtown and Bayview, *Seven Year Itch* at Shea's, *Sign of the Pagan* at the Prince of Wales and Parliament, and a super triple-header at the little Rio, *Gypsy Colt*, *Trapped*, and *Destination Gobi*. People could see the movies with their cars at Toronto's four drive-ins: the 400, North-West, North-East, and Scarboro.

Oh, and just how much did someone pay for my car back in 1955? Exactly $3,063.62 including options (two-speed automatic, GM radio, nail guard), delivery, and taxes.

July 21, 2002

Queen's Quay: Before and After

One of the great summer treats when I was a kid growing up in downtown Toronto was being taken over to the Island. By the way, we never called it Toronto Island or Toronto Islands. Nope, it was simply "the Island," singular, even though it has about thirty of them. And getting there wasn't half the fun. For me it was *all* the fun.

The TTC's big streetcars, often pulling trailers, would transport us to the old ferry docks that back then were located west of the foot of Bay Street. That was after the streetcar turned in the loop at York Street so we passengers could get off on the south side of Queen's Quay. Safer that way. Then, after paying the required fare (in TTC tickets, remember?) we'd enter the waiting area with 2 million others (or so it seemed on those hot, muggy Toronto days). Eventually, the gate would roll back, someone would below over the PA, "Next boat to Centre Island," and we'd all push and shove and squeeze our way onto one of Centre Island ferries. The horn would blow (scaring the life out of the uninitiated who'd never taken this voyage before), the old ferry would shudder, and off we'd go.

Now, most of my fellow travellers were entranced by the view, the Island getting larger in front of us, the city getting smaller behind us. I'd say "at the pointy end" and "at the other end" except the Island boats are double-ended so the only one who knows where we're going is the captain, who has disappeared up the steel stairway to that mysterious place one floor above the rest of us.

Looking west on Queen's Quay, with the 1928 Terminal Warehouse Building, complete with its once familiar White Rose sign up top.

Same view today. The Terminal Warehouse Building is still with us thanks to a $50-million restoration program completed in 1983. Now the site of shops, restaurants, and offices, luxury condominiums replace my White Rose sign. A TTC streetcar on the Harbourfront line (which opened a dozen years ago, is that possible?) makes its way to Union Station.

For me, the mystery wasn't up top. Nope, it was through that door over there that had a sign on it commanding that "Authorized Persons Only" could enter or exit. I'd stare at the door, wishing it open, and sometimes my wish would come true. From somewhere within, a crew member, enveloped in a cloud of oily mist, would emerge to the sound of a roaring diesel engine. Ah, to be able to descend into that marvellous place called the Engine Room. What was even more fascinating was the fact that this guy probably got paid for whatever it was he did down there.

Something else I distinctly remember, this time while approaching the city on the return trip. There, on top of the old Terminal Warehouse Building, was a huge sign, usually back-lit by the late afternoon sun. On the sign was a huge white rose made up of a zillion little light bulbs. They'd light up, starting from the centre then swirling outward until the rose was fully illuminated. The sign was an ad for the White Rose brand of automotive oils and fuels.

The history of the brand is from a time when it looked as if Canada would be a major player in the oil and gas business. White Rose's distant parent was the Canadian Oil Refining Company, one of our nation's earliest petroleum producers. That pioneer Western Ontario enterprise was eventually bought out by the National Refining Company — usually abbreviated EN-AR-CO — of Cleveland, Ohio.

In 1938, White Rose became Canadian once again under the ownership of Nesbitt Thomson, one of Canada's oldest and most successful investment companies and now part of BMO Nesbitt Burns. Eleven years earlier Nesbitt Thomson had created another popular Canadian petroleum retailer, McColl Frontenac. The latter's most celebrated product was Red Indian gasoline, a brand name that today would be viewed as politically incorrect.

In 1964, White Rose was acquired by the mighty Shell organization, and soon the familiar rose emblem wilted into oblivion.

July 28, 2002

Off to Market We Go

So you think we've got traffic problems these days? It would appear from this half-century-old photo that traffic jams have been with us for some time. This view looks east along Front Street toward Jarvis. Prominent in the photo is what remains of a covered walkway that connected the upper levels of the North and South St. Lawrence markets. Obviously, the traffic congestion that existed even in the market's early days was of sufficient concern to prompt this elevated pedestrian right-of-way.

While traffic congestion around the market may have become a tradition, an even older tradition is shopping at the St. Lawrence Market in the first place. In fact, in exactly three months time, the market will enter its two hundredth year of serving the shopping public.

The proclamation that gave birth to a public market at York (now Toronto) was published in the local newspaper, the *Upper Canada Gazette*, on November 5, 1803. It was signed by Peter Hunter, who succeeded John Simcoe as our province's second lieutenant governor, a post he held from 1799 to 1805.

Hunter's declaration went like this:

> Whereas great prejudice has arisen to the inhabitants
> of the town and township of York from no place or day
> having been set apart or appointed for the exposing

274

publicly for sale cattle, sheep, poultry and other provisions, goods and merchandise brought by merchants, farmers and others for the necessary supply of the said town of York; and whereas great benefit and advantage might be derived to the said inhabitants and others by establishing a weekly market within that town at a place and on a day certain for the purpose aforesaid; know all men that I do ordain a public open market to be held on Saturday each and every week during the year on a certain plot or piece of land within that town consisting of five acres and a half ...

Looking east on Front Street toward Jarvis, 1953.

What followed was a rambling and boringly precise description of the proposed market site, which, in simple terms, was to be located on property bounded by King, Jarvis, Front, and Church streets. Frequent visitors to today's market will notice that Hunter's original site did not include what is now known as the South Market. In addition, only about half of his site is now used for a market (we call it the North Market) and the St. Lawrence Hall, the latter having been erected on the ruins of city buildings swept away as a result of the great fire of 1849.

For years a variety of produce companies occupied buildings that were erected on the rest of Hunter's historic block. When the new

Same view today. Note part of the St. Lawrence Market name at top right of both views. In the distance, some of the historic buildings on the north side of Front Street east of Jarvis can be seen.

Ontario Food Terminal opened in south Etobicoke in 1954 much of the pressure was taken off the market area; these ancillary buildings were demolished and a large parking lot built. In the early 1980s the two condominium buildings on the north side of Front and east side of Church (the western part of Hunter's original market square) were constructed.

What is now the South Market had originally been the site of Toronto's first purpose-built City Hall. The old Town Hall at King and Jarvis had been pressed into use as a City Hall by default when incorporation was achieved in 1834. A police station and other municipal operations were also on the site as were some market activities. When a new City Hall opened at the top of Bay Street in 1899, the Front and Jarvis site reverted almost entirely to market uses. Part of the old building was kept and incorporated into the South Market that occupies the site today.

August 4, 2002

Consummating the Union

Hands up all of you who will be celebrating your seventy-fifth birthday this year. Congratulations! You're in good company. A couple of other city landmarks will also be seventy-five in 2002. The Princes' Gates down at the CNE will reach that illustrious plateau later at the end of this month, and hopefully the Ex will celebrate the event in some appropriate fashion. A more immediate special anniversary is that of Toronto's Union Station, which is presently celebrating its seventy-fifth birthday. It actually has two birthdays, August 6 and 11. The station was opened, ceremoniously at least, by the Prince of Wales on August 6, 1927 (Edward, his brother George, and their entourage were the only patrons that particular day). Another five days would pass before the travelling public had its chance to use the city's new railway station for the first time.

Now, I don't know whether the timing was planned or not, but just days before the station's seventy-fifth birthday, Toronto City Council gave the station the nicest present it could when it approved an agenda with the Union Pearson Group Inc. that, if successful, would see major changes to both the look and operation of Union Station. I can only hope that this undertaking will progress more rapidly than did the plans to build the station in the first place.

The idea of building a new main railway station to replace the badly outdated facility then in use can be traced back to the days

277

Toronto's new Union Station under construction, 1916.

immediately following the Great Fire of April 1904. While the conflagration had dealt a major financial and structural blow to the businesses and buildings in city's downtown core area (in fact, some
believed that Toronto would now become the province's second most
important city, with nearby Hamilton taking the lead) there was a silver lining associated with the disaster. The fire had destroyed almost all
of the structures on the south side of Front Street, and now the way was
clear to build that elusive new railway station.

But that hope was to remain just a hope as the two railways
involved (the Grand Trunk and Canadian Pacific: together they made
it a "union" station) began dragging their feet. The location of the new
facility was okay, but it was the way the trains would get to and from the
station that caused concern. Tracks on an elevated viaduct, with bridges
over the city's main north-south streets to and from the harbour, was the
Grand Trunk's desire. However, the CPR felt this method would create
real problems for its waterfront freight yards. Another factor was
whether or not the station should be a terminal, as it would be if the
tracks stub-ended in the new station, or just another through station
with elevated tracks entering the building at one end and exiting at the
other. Back then, when railway tracks were the superhighways of the
day, this distinction was an important factor in establishing a city's status. Having a railway terminal, as the CPR wanted, was more prestigious
by far. After all, wasn't it was Grand Central Terminal, not Grand
Central Station, and didn't we all want to be like New York City?

Four years later things were all ready to roll — except, that is, for the trains.

There was another sticking point. The railways resisted the way payment for the required $6-million viaduct was to be allocated: two-thirds was to come from the railways, while only one-third was to be paid by the city. And the CPR certainly didn't like the Grand Trunk-designed station. In fact, it tried to pull an end run by announcing that the CPR would build its very own station on north Yonge Street (which it did but only used for a few years). That CPR North Toronto Station is presently undergoing major renovations. So there it was. Everyone wanted a new station, but the financial arrangements, the track layout, and company rivalries precluded any work actually starting. The federal government even ordered the railways to get on with it, but that 1905 directive was ignored. Finally, in 1914 work began on the new building, and two years later, December 8, 1916, Building Permit #23544 was issued for the construction of the "Union Station Main Building and East Wing, estimated cost $2.8 million." (When all the bills were in that estimate had become $6 million.)

Some four years later the magnificent new station ("You build your railway stations like we built cathedrals in England," the prince is reported to have said at the official opening) was ready for business, but that darned viaduct was still a problem. More time went by before limited passenger service was possible on this day exactly seventy-five years ago. Full service didn't begin until the viaduct was completed in early 1930 (at a revised cost of $26 million), and to ensure that the railways were treated fairly the first two trains were both inbound, CPR's from Peterborough and CNR's (successor to the Grand Trunk) from Stratford. In all, nearly a quarter of a century had gone by between the time Toronto's Union Station was first ordered built and its final completion. One can only hope its birthday present will ready to open in less time than that.

August 11, 2002

History of Our Brave Mounted Police

Over the summer a couple of new books were published, both of which would be welcome additions to any local history buff's library. The first book has a distinct Toronto focus, while the second is Ontario-wide in its scope. Bill Wardle is a staff sergeant with the Toronto Police Service and is presently assigned to 33 Division in Don Mills. But for most of his twenty-five-year career with the police force he was with the Mounted Unit, where he participated in numerous musical rides, police horse shows, and international competitions and was the founder of the Mounted Unit Drill Team.

Usually the public only sees the Mounted Unit in these "public relations" roles or in parades where everything is presented to educate and entertain. But there's more to being a member of the Mounted Unit, things like the often dangerous crowd control duty or the lonely patrolling of an unpopulated part of the city. The history of Toronto Police Service's Mounted Unit has a rather interesting beginning. Prior to March 1886 there was no such unit, but that's not to say there weren't any mounted police. It was just that a police officer on a horse only appeared when one was needed and only after the steed had been rented from a local livery stable. In fact, it wasn't until several mounted officers were deployed during the often chaotic three-day labour disruption involving the city's privately owned street railway company and its employees in March 1886 that the true worth of policemen

281

Courtesy City of Toronto Archives

Constable Leary helps a lost child at the CNE sometime in the 1930s. The officer's mount looks concerned as well. Note the old grandstand, which was destroyed by fire in 1946, in the background.

and police horses working in unison was conclusively demonstrated.

It was soon thereafter that Chief Constable Dennis Draper convinced the city fathers of the day to approve the establishment of Toronto's first mounted unit. It would consist of seven specially trained officers and the requisite mounts and saddlery. In addition, council approved the purchase of another eight sets of saddlery so that if and when the need arose eight more officers with at least some riding expertise could mount horses from a contracted livery and enter the fray. The author has a passion for the history of the unit in which he served for so many years. This passion is evident in his new book, on which he toiled (in his off time, I might add) for several years.

In *The Mounted Squad: An Illustrated History of the Toronto Mounted Police, 1886–2000* (ISBN 1-55041-631-6) Bill documents, through the use of entertaining text and fascinating photos (many in colour), a year-to-year accounting of the numerous events, both calm and chaotic, at which the mounted unit helped "serve and protect." Also included in the book are stories about many of the proud officers who served with the Mounted Unit over the years. The acquisition and care of police horses, the equipment and regalia, the intricacies of the famous Musical Ride, the special qualities of some of the mounts, as well as the names of many of the horses (Dorothy, Trillium, and No Good to mention just three) are some of the other subjects covered in this encyclopedia of a book. The book is available in some bookstores or directly from the Canadian Mounted Police Association. Call 416-931-4479 for details.

The building where Toronto volunteer fireman William Thornton was fatally injured still stands on the south side of King Street just east of Church.

The second book is on a more sombre subject. *Their Last Alarm* by Mississauga firefighter Robert Kirkpatrick (ISBN 1-894263-61-8) honours the memories of the nearly three hundred Ontario firemen who have lost their lives in the line of duty since the first recorded fatality more than a century and a half ago.

Many Ontario municipalities have lost firefighters over the years (Peterborough lost three in one fire in 1951, the Iroquois volunteer department lost five in a train accident in 1981), but Toronto, being the province's largest city and having the largest fire fighting force, also has the dubious distinction of having the largest number of fatalities. There was the tragic McIntosh Feed Company fire of 1902 (five firemen lost), the ENARCO oil barge disaster of July 1934 (three firemen lost), and, while not specifically in the City of Toronto, the loss of five volunteer firemen of the Kingsway-Lambton brigade during Hurricane Hazel, which struck the city hard. Three Etobicoke firemen lost their lives at the Kimberly-Clark warehouse blaze in 1978. But not all fatalities occurred at the fire scene. Two members of the Scarborough department died in a traffic accident at St. Clair and Warden avenues in 1960. Both the Etobicoke and Scarborough departments became part of Toronto Fire Services in 1998.

Historically, Toronto was also the hometown of the first of the province's firemen to die in the line of duty. When William Thornton joined the city brigade in the 1840s it was still a volunteer organization (a full-time paid Toronto force didn't come about until 1874). On November 22, 1848, while attending a fire in a row of brick structures on King Street just across from St. James' Cathedral, fireman Thornton was struck on the head by some falling debris. He was removed from the site to the nearby Church Street fire hall, where he received treatment for a fractured skull. Thornton, who lived with his mother and sisters, failed to respond to treatment (what little there was back in those days) and died two days later. His memory is honoured on the recently dedicated the Fallen Firefighter Memorial located at # 9 Fire Hall on Queen's Quay West. Incidentally, the author of this book assisted with the historical accuracy of the names listed on this impressive monument.

August 18, 2002

In 2003, the Toronto Fire Services recognized William Thornton's final resting place in St. James' Cemetery with this commemorative headstone.

Enter the Princes' Gates

This coming Friday, one of the city's true landmarks will celebrate its seventy-fifth anniversary. Admittedly, to describe something as a landmark when it's a mere seventy-five years old might be considered a stretch, especially to those who were born in a European or Asian country. In fact, I well remember a tour I gave here in Toronto just days after returning from a visit with my wife to what is now the Czech Republic, her native country. There we visited a church built in the year 900. Back in Toronto, one of the highlights of my tour was to point out to the group as we walked through the CNE grounds a few of our "ancient" monuments: the Scadding Cabin, Press Building, and Horticultural Building of 1794, 1905, and 1907, respectively.

Nevertheless, as one wise sage in the group told me, "If your buildings don't reach a hundred years of age, they'll never reach two hundred." As for the structure that on August 30 will be a step closer to being "ancient," it too is in the CNE grounds. Originally conceived as part of an imposing new eastern entrance to the sprawling grounds of the Canadian National Exhibition, the home of one of the world's great annual fairs, this new structure was anointed, on the drawing boards at least, with the grandiose title of The Diamond Jubilee of Confederation Gates. The "Diamond" part of the title referred to the fact that the year in which the new entrance was to be completed would, in fact, be exactly sixty years after the original four provinces

The Princes' Gates shortly before the dedication ceremony of August 30, 1927. Note the absence of the Automotive Building, which would be built in 1929 on land behind this magnificent structure.

(New Brunswick, Nova Scotia, Canada East, and Canada West) confederated to make up the new Dominion of Canada.

The architects of Toronto's new monument were Alfred H. Chapman and J. Morrow Oxley, whose works (the Northern Ontario Building and Sterling Tower on Bay Street, the Toronto Hydro Building on Carlton Street, the Crosse and Blackwell factory — now Much Music — at Bathurst and Front, and the Ontario Government Building at the west end of the Exhibition grounds, now beautifully restored as the Liberty Grand) live on as some of our city's finest buildings.

While work was nearing completion on the new $186,000 project, it was announced that Their Royal Highnesses Prince Edward and Prince George would be pleased to visit that year's annual exhibition as part of their visit honouring the nation's sixtieth anniversary. They were called upon to review the troops on Saturday, August 30, as part of what we now call Warriors' Day. For the first time, Canada's soldiers, sailors, and airmen would enter the grounds through the new gate. The CNE Board of Directors agreed to give the entrance a new name in recognition of the impending visit of the Prince of Wales (the future King Edward VIII, albeit only for a short period) and Prince George (who was killed in 1942 in a plane crash in Scotland). Thus, when the new entrance was officially dedicated by royalty seventy-five years ago this coming Friday it was as the Princes' Gates.

A couple of features of note. Surmounting the central arch is Winged Victory (not the Angel, as many call her), a three-times life-size figure that was originally created in pre-cast concrete. (Several

On August 30, 1927, Prince Edward cuts the ribbon to officially dedicate the new east entrance to the CNE. The other prince in the title "Princes' Gates" stands to his right. Edward had officially opened Toronto's new Union Station earlier that month.

years ago, a severely deteriorated Victory was replaced with an identical figure of composite plastic.) She stands in her "ship of state" surrounded by smaller figures representing industry and agriculture, the trio guiding the future of Canada. Dates carved on the gate identify the year of the first CNE (1879, when the event was known as the Toronto Industrial Exhibition) and the date of the gates' official opening. The nine columns on either side of the central arch represent the provinces in Confederation in 1927. Newfoundland wouldn't join the Dominion for another twenty-two years.

August 25, 2002

Making an Exhibition

It just doesn't seem possible. A couple more days and another edition of the CNE will be just a memory. And if you haven't made the trek to the fair yet this year what are you waiting for? The "Grand Old Lady" still has lots on her plate to serve up. Come on down and have a taste. Just as certain as the last day of the Ex each year falls on Labour Day, the minute the doors close people will come out of the woodwork with declarations that either commend or castigate one of Toronto's longest traditions. Not that there's anything wrong with that. Virtually from the day the first Toronto Industrial Exhibition (the CNE's original name) opened on September 5, 1879, the Ex has been fair game for both congratulations and complaints. And I'm pretty safe in saying that this year will be no different.

Looking through newspapers of years gone by the the there have been no lack of plans, ideas, drawings, maps, proposals, and concepts put forward that if stacked one on the other would be sufficient to build the CNE a new building, or so former general manager David Garrick reckons. Actually, the grand proposal put forward in the early 1920s was one of the few that went off, or should I say into the ground. That proposal saw a flurry of construction that resulted in a succession of new structures: the Ontario Government Building (now Liberty Grand) in 1926, a new eastern entrance that would become known as the Princes' Gates in 1927, the Electrical and Engineering Building in 1928, the

In 1966, the CNE Board of Directors released this concept for revitalizing the west end of the CNE grounds. Note the islands and lagoons, new exhibit buildings, and busy Lake Shore Boulevard rerouted under the grounds in a tunnel.

Automotive Building in 1930, and the Horse Palace one year later. (This last structure, along with the 1922 Coliseum and its ancillary buildings, was built primarily through the influence of officials at the Royal Winter Fair.) A world depression was followed by a world war, and things at the Ex came to a grinding halt. And so it remained until peace and prosperity finally returned. It took a while to get the fair back together (it had been closed from 1942 to 1946 while being used as a military encampment), and in 1948 the new Grandstand was ready for fair-goers, who were returning in droves.

Things continued to look up with a trio of new exhibit buildings added to the grounds during the 1950s and early 1960s: the Food Building in 1954, the Queen Elizabeth Building (which was originally to be called the Womens' Building) in 1957, and the Better Living Centre in 1962. Then, nearly a half-century went by before another new building was added to the grounds, this one the National Trade Centre, which opened in 1997.

That's not to say that in the meantime there hadn't been grandiose plans put forward to revitalize both the buildings and the grounds. One of the most imaginative was put forward by the CNE's Board of

Directors in June 1966. Several of the ideas in that nine-hundred-page report included extending the CNE grounds east to Bathurst Street where a mammoth new hotel would be built on the Maple Leaf baseball stadium site, constructing an Olympic-size swimming pool at the far west end of the grounds, rerouting the Lake Shore Boulevard so it ran in a tunnel under the CNE, building a new convention and exhibit building in the middle of the grounds with a million car parking garage nearby, and creating a series of man-made islands that would be strung out along the south shoreline of the CNE. This last was to be known as Festival Gardens, and many compared this attraction with Tivoli Gardens in Copenhagen; the report described it as "a delightful combination of flowers, sound, water, lights, music and elegant food."

While nothing happened with any of these ideas, interestingly those man-made islands did appear years later as part of something called Ontario Place, a new provincial attraction that opened in 1971, some five years after the CNE report was released. Coincident with the opening of its new attraction-in-the-water the province vacated the CNE's Ontario Government Building. Since then the future of this lovely old structure has been uncertain to say the least, but now seems to be assured thanks to the Liberty Grand people.

There were a couple of not-so-bright ideas in that CNE report. Plans called for the move of Fort York back the water's edge, where, some experts claimed, it was originally located (forgetting once again that years of landfilling had only made it appear to have moved inland). The 1841 Marine Museum (a.k.a. Stanley Barracks or the New Fort), or at least what's left of one of the city's oldest landmarks, was also to be moved so it would be closer to the repositioned "old" fort. I wonder what ideas will surface after this year's fair has concluded.

September 1, 2002

What Might Have Been

Okay, let's pretend we're walking along Queen Street West. There's the Eaton Centre over there on the right, the old Robert Simpson store, now the Bay, on the left. The only thing left to remind us of a time when this place was called Simpson's are those backward letter "S"s etched in the windows on the second floor and the soaring Simpson Tower ahead of us at the corner, an appendage to the main store that was built in the late 1960s. Across the street is our fabulous "Old" City Hall that would have vanished had the first Eaton Centre scheme been approved. As proof that the city has matured in some respects, the old building, once despised by many, is now being treated to a major program of restoration and repair. And will those grotesques on the clock tower reappear? Stay tuned.

Crossing over Bay Street, the next structure of significance that we see on our walk is Toronto's "New" City Hall. It was built to a design selected in 1958 from the more than five hundred entries submitted during an international competition that drew concepts from architects in forty-two different countries. The winning architect was New York City's I.M. Pei and Associates.

Whoa!! Back up!! I.M. Pei and Associates? That's not right. The architect of Toronto's new City Hall was Viljo Revell ... wasn't it? Well, yes he was, but it could have been Ioeh Ming Pei (who subsequently did the Bank of China in Hong Kong and the Rock and Roll Hall of Fame

Toronto City Hall, or at least as it would have been had the design jury selected this I.M. Pei idea over that of winner Viljo Revell.

This design by Barnes, Gilbert, and Hewitt was intriguing, but it didn't make it past the first cut.

in Cleveland) if the five internationally recognized individuals judging the Toronto competition had come up with a different selection than the one they did. This possibility makes for interesting speculation.

What if some other design had been chosen, say the one by David Horne, the only Canadian in the list of eight finalists? Or that by Denmark's Gunnlogson and Nielsen, or Australia's John H. Andrews?

Actually that last chap is of interest to Torontonians because he's the same John H. Andrews who is the architect-of-record for the CN Tower. So while John didn't win the competition to design the city's new City Hall, he did return almost two decades later with another of his creations, the CN Tower. Now, just to make sure the record is straight (and to stop those with their fingers on the e-mail "send" button), it was Finnish architect Viljo Revell's design that we recognize today as "New" City Hall. And while we still refer to his remarkable and enduring work as Toronto's "New" City Hall, the building attained the advanced age (for Toronto buildings) of thirty-seven last Friday. Interestingly, when Revell's design was selected on September 26, 1958, some referred to it as "horrid", "odd," and "phony, like most modern art."

September 15, 2002

Dental College Endures

Remember the old joke, "What time is it when you go to the dentist? Why, it's tooth-hurty, of course." (Get it? For those who don't, pretend I said 2:30.) Now I don't know whether this was just a coincidence or not, but for many years the Royal College of Dental Surgeons (RCDS) was located in a grand old building at the northeast corner of College and Huron streets. Why do I wonder whether this location was a coincidence? Because for many years the building's street address was "tooth-hurty," oh, all right, 230. What brought the subject of the Dental College to mind was my recent purchase of an old postcard that showed this same building on a tree-lined College Street with a streetcar waiting out in front at the Huron Street car stop.

It was obvious to me that the view was perfect for one of those "then and now" pairings. After snapping the "now" view, I decided to learn more about the building and contacted Dr. Anne Dale, archivist for the Faculty of Dentistry at the University of Toronto. Dr. Dale advised me that the training of dentists by the Royal College of Dental Surgeons here in Toronto began in the late 1860s, and though a lack of funds closed the school for a short time, by 1875 teaching was underway in two rented rooms in a building at Church and Court streets.

Over the next couple of decades classes were held in various rented downtown locations. However, that all changed when on October

Postcard view looking east along College Street shortly after the opening of the Royal College of Dental Surgeons building in the fall of 1909.

The old building still stands and the streetcar still stops at its front door, 2002.

12, 1909, the school moved into its very own building at College and Huron streets, a state-of-the-art structure designed by the prominent city architectural firm of Burke, Horwood and White. At first the school's address was 240 College Street, but by 1932 (and for reasons unknown) this address was changed to 230. (I wonder if anyone back then saw the humour associated with the change?)

More moves were ahead for the school, and in 1959 classes were relocated to the present Faculty of Dentistry building at 124 Edward Street In addition to its teaching function (for dentists and dental hygienists) the faculty has a major commitment to dental research in the fields of dental implantology and periodontal physiology. Now if they could just do something about the sound of my dentist's drill.

We often regard our neighbouring community to the west, the City of Mississauga, as big and bright and shiny. And as such, it's difficult to regard the city as having much in the way of history. But a thorough reading of a recently published hardcover book compiled by the dedicated folks at the Mississauga Heritage Foundation quickly dispels that myth. *Mississauga, the First 10,000 Years* features sixteen chapters (and dozens of photographs) that collectively describe the evolution of the city, starting with its landscape (with emphasis on the Credit River and Rattray Marsh) and its earliest inhabitants (the name *Mississauga* refers to the original Amerindian inhabitants and when translated into English approximates "a river having several mouths"). The book moves on to the city's first European settlers (and the growth of Toronto Township, Streetsville and the Benares farmstead) and the community's maturing with the arrival of the Croats, Portuguese, Chinese, and others who chose Canada, and Mississauga, as their new home. The book is available at several Mississauga bookstores. For specific stores call the Foundation at 905-615- 4415 or visit its website (www.heritagemississauga.com).

September 22, 2002

A Desire for Streetcars

Today is the twenty-third anniversary of an important event in the history of public transportation in Toronto. On this day in 1979, Torontonians were officially introduced to their new streetcar, the Canadian Light Rail Vehicle (or simply CLRV). Although there was a time in the 1970s when many thought Toronto's streetcars were coming to the end of the line, the arrival of the CLRV meant our city would have streetcars well into the future.

Historically, that "streetcar city" characterization was first given to our city on September 11, 1861, when the newly established Toronto Street Railway Co. (TSR) put its new horse-drawn streetcars into service, much to the amazement and satisfaction of the community's 45,000 citizens. Prior to that date getting around town was pretty much done on foot, by horse and buggy, or on the stagecoaches of the city's public transportation pioneer, Henry Burt Williams.

The TSR's new streetcars were a godsend for most people and their popularity soared. Before long tracks were to be found on many of the city's main thoroughfares. The next major operational improvement came in 1892 when a new enterprise, the Toronto Railway Company (TRC), took over the TSR's franchise and, as required by the terms of its contract with the city, began introducing equipment powered by the marvel of the age, electricity. By 1894 the company's horses had all been replaced by something called electrons, mysterious little things

A wooden mock-up of Toronto's new streetcar was displayed at the 1975 CNE. At the close of the fair, the model was transported to the TTC's Hillcrest shops at Bathurst and Davenport.

that were now propelling streetcars of various sizes and shapes all over town. In 1920, the city electorate approved converting the private transportation system into a municipally regulated public service. On September 1, 1921, the new Toronto Transportation Commission (the name was altered to the Toronto Transit Commission coincident with the opening of the Yonge subway in 1954) went into business using hundreds of the older types of streetcar. These were phased out when replacements in the form of the then state-of-the-art Peter Witts began arriving from the Canadian Car and Foundry factory in Montreal. And while a few gasoline buses were starting to appear on various "feeder" routes around town, Toronto was still very much a "streetcar city." In fact, its equipment roster for 1937 boasted more than eight hundred electric vehicles.

The following year saw the Commission make another major commitment to electric vehicle operations with the acquisition of 140 of the new Presidents' Conference Committee streetcars. Over the next few years additional PCC cars were purchased, many of them from American cities where gas and diesel bus manufacturers had done a superb selling job. In 1953, the TTC equipment roster boasted a total of 1,058 streetcars, a number that would decrease slightly with the introduction of subway service the following year. However, even as late as 1960 there were still more that one thousand streetcars on the TTC's books.

But management could see a problem looming. It wouldn't be long before even the venerable PCC car would need to be replaced. TTC staff even went so far as to recommend phasing out streetcars altogether by 1980 and replacing them with buses. A citizens group was quick-

On this day twenty-three years ago the public came out in droves to see and ride the new CLRV streetcars. Peter Witt #2424 (background right) was part of the big event.

ly mustered and did a masterful job of convincing the TTC's hierarchy that such a move would not be in the TTC's best interests. (The oil crisis was still in the future.) In November 1972 the TTC decided to retain streetcar operations, but recognized that to do so, new streetcars would be necessary. So coincident with the decision to keep Toronto a streetcar city, staff was asked to find a replacement vehicle while doing a heavy rebuild of 173 PCCs to help tide things over until the new cars were ready for service.

Some thought the TTC should develop and build that replacement vehicle itself; however, that was not to be. A number of potential manufacturers worldwide were contacted and several designs proposed with one possibility appearing at the 1975 edition of the CNE. The fair had only been underway for a few days when the TTC announced it had placed an order for two hundred new Canadian Light Rail Vehicles with the Ontario (later Urban) Transportation Development Corp. The first six prototype cars (four less than first proposed) were built by the Swiss Industrial Company, a long-time manufacturer of railway rolling stock, with the remaining 190 cars produced in the Hawker Siddeley Canada's Thunder Bay, Ontario, factory.

The new streetcars arrived in Toronto over a four-year period, the first on a freezingly cold December 29, 1977, the last on November 19, 1981. Torontonians saw their first new streetcar, #4000, at the 1978

Centennial Edition of the CNE. A ceremonial service introduction took place at the Humber streetcar loop on September 29 of the following year, with Toronto's new streetcar entering revenue service the next day on the "507" Long Branch route. After some rough moments Toronto was to remain a streetcar city.

September 29, 2002

That Was Then, This Is Now

Nothing exemplifies the remarkable growth of Toronto better than photographs taken decades apart from similar vantage points. Contrasting "then and now" photos that are featured from time to time in this column often evoke the comment, "Are you sure both pictures are of the same place?" In most cases you just have to take my word for it, but there is one part of the city in which, though the changes have been remarkable, at least one element of the view has remained constant since it first appeared on the skyline in the late 1920s. That element is the Royal York Hotel (now officially identified as the Fairmont Royal York in recognition of the hotel's affiliation with the Canadian-controlled Fairmont family of hotels and resorts, the largest operator of luxury hotels and resorts in North America). The Royal York was there then and it's there now, as the "then" and "now" photos accompanying this column will attest.

The genesis of Toronto's Royal York Hotel can be traced back to the early Roaring Twenties, when the federal government decided to bring together a number of bankrupt and nearly bankrupt railways, giving the new operation the name Canadian National Railways. It was then that Canadian Pacific Railway's energetic president Edward Beatty (whose birthplace in Thorold, Ontario, was recently recognized with an Ontario Heritage Foundation plaque) decided to meet his company's new competition head-on by making major improvements

301

Credit: Toronto Port Authority Archives

Toronto's skyline in early 1929 is dominated by the new Royal York Hotel. The large boathouse in the foreground still survives as Pier 6, now a coffee shop and souvenir outlet.

Similar view today.

to CPR's trio of existing hotels (the Chateau Frontenac, Chateau Lake Louise, and the Banff Springs Hotel) and by building two new hotels, the Hotel Saskatchewan in Regina and an as yet unnamed hotel in the nation's largest English-speaking city (as our city was then described), Toronto. In fact, it was Beatty himself who gave Toronto's new hotel the name Royal York. It's recorded that he selected the title from statements made by Toronto's founder John Graves Simcoe, who, during his time in Upper Canada (Ontario) often referred to his new settlement as "our Royal Town Of York."

Simcoe, who didn't like the sound of aboriginal words, selected the name York to honour King George III's second eldest son, Frederick, the Duke of York. That title was subsequently changed back to the original Toronto when the town was elevated to city status in 1834, long after Simcoe had departed the scene. The site selected for Toronto's new hotel was an obvious choice, across from the city's new railway station, which had been paid for, in part and grudgingly, by the CPR. A special feature to help the travel-weary railway passengers would be an underground tunnel connecting the hotel and the station. That tunnel still exists and is a pioneer component of the vast PATH system that snakes its way under the streets of the modern downtown Toronto.

While the site was an obvious choice, its selection did result in the loss of one of the city's landmark structures, the old Queen's Hotel, one of the city's oldest hostelries that began simply as a row of houses on the north side of an often muddy Front Street. It's hard to say if any citizens' groups of the day protested its demolition in 1927. The Royal York, oops Fairmont Royal York Hotel opened to the public on June 11, 1929. Hey, that means it'll be seventy-five in just a couple of years. I wonder if they're planning a party?

October 6, 2002

Spad-ee-na, Spad-eye-na?

I often recall sitting and chatting with my grandmother about the Toronto that she knew so well. Of the many stories she told me, the one that still brings a smile whenever my travels take me anywhere near Spadina Avenue is how, when she was a young woman, she knew where people lived by the way they pronounced the word *Spadina*. To those who were well-heeled and resided north of Bloor it was always Spad-ee-na, while to the less affluent south of Bloor it was Spad-eye-na. And for those who lived over in a still-ungentrified Cabbagetown, and really didn't give a darn anyway, it was pronounced Spad-eye-ner.

While the vast majority of citizens continue to use the Spad-eye-na pronunciation, it was the citizenry living north of Bloor who had it right. That's because the word evolved from the First Nation's term *Ishapadenah*, a word that meant "a hill" or "a sudden rise in the land." In the Toronto context the word was used to describe the hill on which pioneer Torontonian Dr. William Warren Baldwin would erect his "suburban" residence in 1818.

In recognition of the Native word that described the site of his new house, the good doctor anglicized Ishapadenah and named his new abode Spadina. In modern Toronto terms Baldwin's place was located where the more modern (1866) Spadina House now stands and just steps to the northeast of our famous, but troubled, Casa Loma. As for the pronunciation of the word Ishapadenah, author Austin Seton

304

There's been a branch of the Canadian Imperial Bank of Commerce at the northwest corner of Spadina Avenue and College Street almost as long as there have been streetcars in Toronto. This branch (then part of the Canadian Bank of Commerce organization) opened in 1888. Streetcars arrived in Toronto in 1861, operating on Spadina Avenue for the first time in 1878 and on College some fifteen years later.

Similar view, October 13, 2002.

Thompson revealed in his magnificent book *Spadina: A Story of Old Toronto* that the use of the hard "i" was not a characteristic of the native peoples' language. Therefore, the word would have been pronounced Ishapad-ee-nah, which was altered by the doctor to Spadina and, obviously, pronounced Spad-ee-nah.

Today's Spadina Avenue, that is the portion between Bloor and Queen streets, was originally laid out, it's said, so that Dr. Baldwin could see the bay from his house on the hill. While most main streets were created 66 feet in width (a Gunter's chain), Spadina was carved through the forest two chains wide, making it 132 feet in width. Its present 160-foot width is a more recent alteration. Originally, the stretch of Spadina from Queen to the edge of Toronto Bay (then just south of Front Street) was known as Brock Street; it wasn't incorporated into the Spadina Avenue right-of-way we know today until 1884. Spadina Road, the narrower extension of Spadina Avenue from Bloor Street to Davenport Road, was created in the 1870s when Dr. Baldwin's grandson, Robert Baldwin, began subdividing his grandfather's original land holdings. Spadina Road served at the new subdivision's easternmost boundary.

October 13, 2002

Will Plans Fly This Time?

Earlier this month the Toronto Port Authority (TPA) announced a new plan that, if implemented, would go far in ensuring a viable future for the beleaguered Toronto City Centre Airport at the west end of Toronto Island. The TPA plan includes the creation of a second regional airline (to supplement service now provided by Air Canada), the building of a new, state-of-the-art passenger terminal, and the construction of a bridge connecting the airport with the mainland. While the first two components of the plan may be new, the concept of a "fixed link" certainly is not. In fact, a review of the Island's history reveals that a fixed link existed right from the start. That's because Toronto Island began life as a long, sandy peninsula with its east end connected to the mainland in the vicinity of the modern Cherry Beach via a narrow isthmus. This, the original fixed link, vanished during a violent storm in the spring of 1858. It wasn't long after the conversion from peninsula to island took place that people began to agitate for some sort of fixed connection. Back then many families found the cost of getting to the Island prohibitive due to the cost of riding to and from the waterfront on the city's privately operated streetcar system plus the added cost of the round-trip fare to the Island on the privately operated ferry boats.

One idea to make the day's outing a little cheaper was presented in 1885 and was, interestingly enough, in the form of a "streetcar-only" bridge that would give passengers a cheaper one-fare access to the

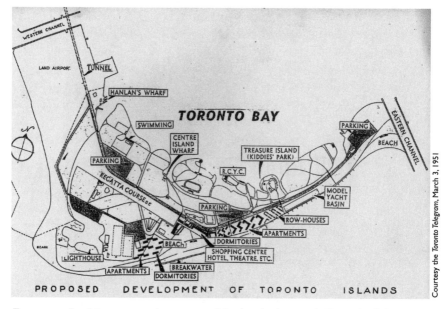

PROPOSED   DEVELOPMENT   OF   TORONTO   ISLANDS

Courtesy the *Toronto Telegram*, March 3, 1951

Fortunately, this proposal, approved by both the city's Board of Control and the Toronto Harbour Commission a half-century ago, went nowhere. If it had, today's island would have a shopping centre, hotel, apartment buildings, row houses, and a highway with parking lots all accessed by a tunnel under the Western Channel.

Island. While nothing came of this particular idea, the fixed link concept never really went away. In fact, the original Toronto Harbour Commission waterfront plan of 1912 even included a lift bridge over the East Gap that, if built, would reinstate the original fixed link destroyed during the storm of 1858. A century later there was even talk of the TTC operating an aerial ride using enclosed cars, like those used at some ski resorts, to carry people over the West Gap.

Again nothing happened. In fact, the closest we ever came to getting that elusive fixed link began to take shape exactly sixty-seven years ago this month. That's when the Dominion Construction Co. began work on a $976,264 contract it was awarded by the Conservative government under R.B. Bennett to construct a 2,200-foot-long tunnel running from the foot of Bathurst Street, under the West Gap, to just south of the proposed new Island Airport site. It would be 15 feet in height, have a pair of 7 foot, 6 inch-wide pedestrian sidewalks and a 20-foot-wide roadway. Vehicles would proceed no further than the airport's parking lots.

Just days after work began, the Conservative Party was defeated by the Mackenzie King Liberals, and on October 30, 1935, the new prime minister ordered all work suspended (shades of the Conservative cancellation of the Arrow project twenty-four years later). Arguments for and against the fixed link continued for almost a year, and in the summer of 1936 a portion of the tunnel excavation already in place at the foot of Bathurst Street was filled in. So, you'll pardon me if I'm a bit skeptical about this fixed link thing. In fact, I'll believe there is one the day I walk to the Island.

A couple of weeks ago I spoke about the history of Toronto to a friendly group of people in the pretty little community of Collingwood. After my talk I asked if there were any questions. One member of the audience asked if I was aware that a trio of former townships in the area, Tiny, Flos, and Tay, were so named in honour of the three pet lapdogs of Elizabeth Simcoe, the wife of the province's first lieutenant-governor and founder of the modern Toronto, John Graves Simcoe. My answer was that while part of her story was correct, that of the townships being named for dogs, I was pretty sure they weren't the pets of Mrs. Simcoe. But in a moment of brain overload (I need more RAM) I couldn't think of exactly who did own the dogs. A little on-line research and I now have the answer. Since many of the people at the talk read the *Sunday Sun* I hope someone will pass on the information to the lady who presented the question. The owner of the trio of Pekinese was, in fact, Lady Sarah Maitland, wife of Sir Peregrine Maitland, who served from 1818 to 1828 as Upper Canada's fifth lieutenant-governor.

October 20, 2002

Rollin' on Toronto Bay

One of the strangest vessels ever seen on Toronto Bay (or, I suspect, on any other bay for that matter) was the one created by Mr. Frederick Knapp. The story behind Mr. Knapp's so-called roller boat is a fascinating one made even more intriguing by the fact that the photograph accompanying this column, a photo commissioned by the inventor himself to commemorate one of this unique craft's numerous trial voyages on Toronto Bay, was taken exactly 105 years ago this very day, October 30, 1897. Frederick Knapp was born in 1854 and was a resident of Prescott, Ontario. His vocation was that of a lawyer; his passion, that of an inventor. In fact, it was his passion for inventing that resulted in his famous (or as it turned out infamous) roller boat, a strange-looking craft that was intended to roll over waves, no matter their height or intensity.

It has been suggested that Knapp's idea of a boat that would be impervious to wave action was prompted by his admiration of Queen Victoria. It was a well-known fact that his queen refused to travel great distances by boat because of her predisposition to seasickness. Now, if Knapp could invent a vessel that precluded the motions that brought on this distress, Her Majesty would agree to cross the Atlantic and pay a visit her dominion in North America. While in Canada she would no doubt request an audience with this remarkable boat's inventor. There could even be a knighthood in it for Knapp.

"The Knapp Roller Boat   And Its Inventor."

The Roller Boat (with its inventor Frederick Knapp, inset) undergoes trials on Toronto Bay on this very day 105 years ago.

Whatever the reason behind the young lawyer/inventor's decision to build such an unusual craft, his dream caused quite a sensation in the city when work on the roller boat got underway at the Toronto factory of the Polson Iron Works Co., which was located on the waterfront at the foot of Sherbourne Street. (Today the Polson site would be on the west side of the street south of The Esplanade. Interestingly, Polson was also the company that would build the now restored Toronto Island ferry *Trillium* and RCYC passenger launch *Kwasind* in 1910 and 1912, respectively.)

As can be seen in the accompanying photograph, the prototype roller boat was a strange-looking craft, to say the least. Inside the 110-foot-long, 22-foot-diameter outer cylinder was a slightly smaller cylinder in which freight and/or passengers would be carried. Two steam engines, one at either end of the craft, were connected to the outer cylinder in such a way as to cause the latter to rotate (much like a rolling pin when it's rolled over a table). While the outer cylinder did its thing, the inner structure, suspended at either end on huge bearings, remained in a flat plane. Blades affixed to the exterior of the revolving cylinder would catch the water, thereby propelling Knapp's vessel over the water. Theoretically, waves of any magnitude would not be felt on board the craft. The queen would be pleased.

As work progressed, Knapp became more and more enthusiastic, even to the extent of designing a pair of enormous roller boats, the first for the transportation of up to 4 million bushels of grain and the second as a troop carrier for the American government. With hostilities between Spain and the U.S. reaching a crisis point, Knapp was sure this latter vessel would be capable of quickly transporting up to thirty thousand American soldiers, along with hundreds of tons of equipment, from Florida to Cuba. This action would ensure a victory over the Spanish troops who occupied the island and help in the liberation of Cuba. Unfortunately, during trials on Toronto Bay the prototype never lived up to expectations. While the vessel did roll, the speed attained was a major disappointment, and even if the vessel were to be equipped with more powerful engines, it was obvious that a proposed top speed of 60 miles per hour for the larger versions of the roller boat would never be attained. Knapp kept his spirits up, and over the next few years constantly assured everyone that his invention would pay handsome dividends someday. Several attempts were made to improve the vessel's operating characteristics. When they too failed, a plan was put forward to use Knapp's creation as a barge.

Eventually, however, all interest in the vessel — including Knapp's — ceased. All, that is, except that of its builder. One day in the fall of 1907, the long-abandoned hull of the derelict craft broke loose from its moorings in the Polson wharf, wandered along the waterfront, and hit one of the large lake boats. To pay for the damage it caused, the roller boat was sold, fetching a mere $295 for her fittings and another $300 for the hull.

For some reason the hull was never actually claimed, and as the Toronto Harbour Commission continued to create new land across the waterfront the time came when the roller boat was simply in the way. Crews arranged to drag what was left of the roller boat from its resting place in the now landlocked site of the Polson wharf to the new waterfront taking shape at the foot of Parliament Street. It was here that the revolutionary craft became just so much landfill. And while its exact location is not known for certain, it's quite possible that the remnants of Mr. Knapp's roller boat are under the Gardiner Expressway, as close to transportation as it ever got.

October 27, 2002

Say Goodbye to the Past

Can you imagine our city without its stately "Old" City Hall or its majestic Union Station? I can't, but were it not for the timely intrusion of a group of ordinary citizens both of these Toronto landmarks would exist today only in photographs.

Other structures, all touchstones of Toronto's distant past, have also been saved from oblivion by a variety of organizations, quasi-government foundations, and ordinary citizens. Campbell House, Fort York, the St. Lawrence Hall, the Elgin, Winter Garden, and Royal Alexandra theatres, and Toronto's first Post Office are just a few of the structures that would simply be footnotes in the city's history books had some group or individual not cared.

While we're better today at recognizing and preserving our past, unless steps are taken quickly another resource, this time of both city and provincial significance, will itself be part of history. This time the threat has been imposed (not for the first time mind you) on an important archeological site, that of Upper Canada's (after 1867, Ontario's) first parliament buildings, which stood south and west of the busy Front and Parliament streets intersection.

While it's far too late to do anything about the actual brick structures that occupied this site (they stood here from 1797 until destroyed by fire during the American invasion of our town in April 1813) remnants of those same buildings plus other related artifacts have been

Courtesy *From Front Street to Queen's Park* by Eric Arthur, McClelland & Stewart, 1979.

Just six years after Ontario (then called Upper Canada) came into being in 1791 this pair of brick structures was erected on the south side of Front Street near Parliament (thus the name of the latter street).

What remains of one of the most important complexes of buildings from Ontario's past lies under this mixture of nondescript buildings.

uncovered. This has prompted many citizens and several government agencies to advocate acquisition of the site to prevent further desecration of the property. So urgent is their appeal that unless something is done by the end of this month construction of a car dealership on the site will begin, and what traces of our very beginnings remain will simply be hauled away.

However, if the property comes under public jurisdiction ways can then be developed to interpret the site and tell the story of our province's, and our city's, fascinating beginnings. It would appear that at this late date the best course of action would be for the provincial Ministry of Culture to step in and assume leadership in helping preserve what little there may still be of these historic buildings.

* While a new European car dealership has arisen on a portion of the old Parliament Building site, there is still hope that at some time in the near future the true historical value of the site can be realized.

TTC's first passenger

Little did Robert Ferguson realize that when he boarded streetcar #726 and deposited his fare he became the first of nearly 24 billion passengers who since that early September 1 morning eighty-one years ago have taken "The Better Way." Ferguson, a porter at the King Edward Hotel, had just finished his late afternoon shift and was headed home. The streetcar he boarded at the King and Yonge corner was a Belt Line car operating on a route that would have taken him west on King then north on Spadina, where he would have left the car at the Bloor corner. Ferguson would have continued his early morning trip home by walking a couple of blocks west along Bloor before turning south at Brunswick Avenue, entering the house at #285 where he boarded with a Mr. Baylis.

While the streetcar he boarded hadn't changed in any way, nor had the route he travelled each night, the fare he had to pay was different. And significantly so. The night before, Ferguson had paid just a nickel, but with the birth of the new municipally owned Toronto Transportation Commission less than a minute before he got on the streetcar, a new night fare of fifteen cents cash had been instituted.

Riders using the new TTC later that morning would also pay more. The new daytime cash fare had also been increased, from a nickel to seven cents. Both these increases were necessary in order that the new Commission could embark on a multi-million-dollar program to buy new streetcars (Peter Witts), replace badly deteriorated and dangerous trackwork, upgrade existing car houses, and erect a modern repair shop. And, perhaps most the most important reason of all, to create a one-fare city-wide public transit system. The days of making money with little or no regard for the plight of the poor passengers would vanish with the creation of the TTC. Incidentally, that night fare wasn't abolished until 1931 when all adult cash fares became ten cents.

The reason for this brief look back is to inform readers of the TTC's 24 Billionth Rider Contest. While it's impossible to tell who that 24 billionth rider might be, the Commission wants to celebrate anyway and will be awarding some great prizes to the twenty-four riders who, in the opinion of the judges, submit the twenty-four best stories related to "Taking the Better Way." By the way, are there any members of Mr. Ferguson's family still around? If so, please drop me a line.

November 3, 2002

Come Dance With Me

For anyone who remembers dancing to the sounds of the big bands, a marvellous new book has just been published that'll bring back memories no matter whether your favourite dance hall was in Tweed, Tamworth, Timmins, or Toronto. In compiling material for his book *Let's Dance* (Natural Heritage Books, $26.95), author Peter Young sought help through a note he sent to the "Letter to the Editor" section in various newspapers across the province.

According to Peter, the response was overwhelming, with hundreds of readers eager to share their memories with him and, following the publication of the book, with us.

Of special interest are the many dance halls in and around Toronto, the vast majority of which existed until now only as sweet memories. In Peter's new book, they come alive once again, this time in words and photos. Remember the Casino at Centre Island, the Fallingbrook Pavilion and the Balmy Beach Club, the Silver Slipper on Riverside Drive, the Embassy Club on Bloor, and the big dance tent at the annual CNE? They're all in the book plus dozens more. A great read!

November 10, 2002

The Palace Pier, one of Toronto's most popular dance halls, seen here jutting out into the lake at the mouth of the Humber River. In went up in flames in early 1963, about a decade after this photo was taken. Note also the Supertest gas station and at the centre top a portion of Brooker's drive-in restaurant, one of the first in the city.

The Palais Royale opened as a dance hall on Lake Shore Boulevard West in 1922. Thankfully, it's still in business. This rare photo, which was sent to me by a reader, shows the building when Walter Dean was still making his remarkable Sunnyside Torpedo canoes in the basement.

Origins of the Sheppard Subway Line

This time next week Torontonians will be able to travel on the city's newest subway line. Construction of the 6.4-kilometre Sheppard subway officially began on June 23, 1994, when the provincial premier of the day, Bob Rae, drove a jackhammer into the pavement near the Sheppard-Doris avenues intersection. Interestingly, this momentous event occurred a little more than forty years after Toronto's first subway, the Yonge line, opened between Union Station and Eglinton Avenue on March 30, 1954. The origins of the Sheppard line can be traced back to the early 1980s when a variety of Metro Toronto and TTC-sponsored studies recommended reducing the pressure on the downtown core by creating development sub-centres in the suburbs. To do this, several possible transit corridors, including Finch and Eglinton West, were studied, and by 1985 there was general consensus that priority be given to a subway along Sheppard East.

The following year Metro Toronto Council approved "Network 2011," a report that proposed that the construction of a subway running from the Sheppard subway station on the Yonge line easterly to Victoria Park Avenue be the first priority in a twenty-five-year rapid transit expansion strategy. (The Sheppard station had opened in early 1974 as part of the York Mills to Finch extension of the Yonge line.) In 1994 preliminary work began on the new Sheppard line. Three years later a pair of huge tunnel boring machines, nicknamed "Rock" and "Roll," set off

A narrow Sheppard Avenue looking east from Yonge, *circa* 1935.

Southbound Yonge Street traffic approaches the Sheppard intersection in the late 1940s. The streetcar track was that of the North Yonge Railway, a radial line that connected Toronto at the TTC's City Limits terminal with Richmond Hill. Its predecessor was the Toronto and York Metropolitan Radial, which ran as far north as Jackson's Point and Sutton.

on their underground missions to sculpt huge underground subway tunnels, the first pair running westerly from Leslie Street to Yonge. Then, returning to Leslie, they set off easterly, carving extensions to the newly identified (and dollar saving) terminus at Don Mills Road. The 6.4-kilo-metre (4-mile) line is made up of nearly 4 kilometres (2.5 miles) of tunnels plus 2.4 kilometres (1.5 miles) built by the cut-and-cover method. The Don River is crossed via an award-winning bridge structure. The new $933-million subway has five stations, each of which is named for the nearby street intersection. While the selection of these names is a totally practical endeavour, the names are far more interesting if we look at their origins. For instance, the western terminus of the line is at a station called Sheppard-Yonge. It sits atop the existing Sheppard station on the Yonge line and consists of the surnames of both Sir George Yonge, the secretary of war in the cabinet of King George III, and a pioneer family that settled this once forest-covered area more than two centuries ago. The first of the Shepards (or Shepherds or Sheppards; the spelling in early documents varied) was Joseph, who built a log cabin on the northwest corner of the intersection in 1798.

Bayview Avenue began as a narrow pathway cut through the forest some one hundred chains (sixty-six hundred feet or one mile) east of the prime surveyors' line, Yonge Street The road was originally known as the First Concession Road East (of Yonge). Later it became known as the East York Road, as it separated the township from the city. More recently it was changed again, this time to Bayview Avenue, a nice-sounding term that described the view to the south and no doubt made property easier to sell.

Leslie Street is truly historic in nature, as it recalls pioneer businessman George Leslie, who lived in the countryside some two miles east of the young city of Toronto, where he ran a large nursery for many years. The nearby concession road became the road to Leslie's and eventually Leslie Street. Tracing the street northward it becomes Donlands Avenue through East York emerging north of the Don Valley once more as Leslie Street. Don Mills Road (originally the Don Independent Road since land for its construction as an early public improvement was given by nearby farmers) recognizes the flour, grist, woollen, and sawmills on the Don River, of which there were many.

Readers will have noticed that thus far I've identified just four of the five station names. As for the origin of the Bessarion stop, the one between Bayview and Leslie, no one seems to know. Any suggestions?

November 17, 2002

From Footpath to Street

Several weeks ago I wrote about the origins of one of the city's busiest and most interesting thoroughfares, Spadina Avenue. This week I'll focus on another major city street that like Spadina began as a private laneway. In the case of Spadina, the laneway was cut through dense forest by the ubiquitous Dr. William Warren Baldwin, who moved from the comfort of the little Town of York (a small community that in 1834 would be elevated to city status and renamed Toronto) to the escarpment north of the young city. On a site just east of today's Casa Loma, the doctor built a house he called Spadina, an anglicized version of a Native word that translated as "a sudden rise in the land." As reported in early diaries, one of benefits of the laneway that has evolved into Spadina Avenue is that it permitted Baldwin a clear view of the harbour and peninsula (now Toronto Island) almost two miles to the south.

Like Spadina, Jarvis Street also began life as a private driveway. Laid out in 1824, the drive ran north from Lot Street (now Queen Street) to the newly constructed residence of Samuel Peters Jarvis on a hundred-acre farm he had inherited from his father, William. The senior Jarvis had been a good friend and follower of John Graves Simcoe, the town's founder, and as such had been awarded by the Crown a hundred-acre piece of property northwest of the townsite officially described as Park Lot 6 (thus the original name of the street on which it fronted) in the First Concession north of the Bay.

Jarvis Street looking north from Carlton Street *circa* 1935

Same view in 2002. Note the old Havergal school building to the extreme left in both views.

In 1818 William passed away and his Park Lot became the property of his son Samuel. The younger Jarvis was a lawyer and government official and one of the town's most prominent, and interesting (if that's the correct term), citizens. He bore the stigma of having shot and killed a fellow citizen in a duel, one of only two ever contested in York. While Jarvis was automatically charged with the death of Thomas Ridout on July 12, 1817, as a result of the duel (carried out in a clearing not far north of the site of today's Toronto Police Service headquarters on College near Bay) an inquiry determined that all proper protocol had been followed and young Sam Jarvis was soon acquitted.

In 1824, Jarvis built himself a two-storey brick residence on his Park Lot that he called Hazelburn (interestingly, selected as the name of a modern housing co-op just up the street). The original Hazelburn was located just south of the present Jarvis and Shuter intersection and was reached by a long dirt driveway running north from Lot Street to the south. An interesting sidelight to the development of the Jarvis property occurred about this same when Sam and his neighbour to the west, Peter McGill, decided to build a new road between their respective properties. To do so, a narrow strip of land was taken from each Park Lot resulting in a thoroughfare that was, in effect, a mutual driveway. Today we know that mutual driveway as Mutual Street. Years passed and when Jarvis found himself in financial straits he decided to subdivide the hundred-acre Park Lot into building lots to raise money. In 1845 the old house, which stood in the way of progress (not necessarily a modern term), was pulled down. The driveway that led to it was extended north to the Second Concession, today's Bloor Street; thus it was that Jarvis Street, at least the Queen to Bloor portion, was born. To it was added the existing road to the south that ran as New (later Nelson) Street from Lot (Queen) Street to the bay. It had been opened at the time of York's first period of expansion that pushed the town's original western boundary at George Street further west to Peter Street in 1817. More about the street and the Jarvis family can be found in Austin Seton Thompson's marvellous book *Jarvis Street: A Story of Triumph and Tragedy*. In the older of the accompanying photographs we see a still rather residential Jarvis Street north of Carlton Street after a major snowstorm sometime in the mid-1930s. (Photos that come to me from readers are frequently undated.) Visible to the left of the view is the old Havergal College building that was erected in 1898. It later became known as the CBC's Radio Building. (For a time I co-hosted with long-time CBC announcer Harry Manus, a show called *Our Town* from an ancient studio in this old building.) Next to it is one of the stately old residences that lined upper Jarvis. This one was built in 1856 and was for a time the residence of Sir Oliver Mowat, one-time Ontario premier and lieutenant-governor and a father of Confederation. Both these historic structures will be incorporated into the new Radio City condominium complex presently under development with the National Ballet School of Canada filling the two historic structures with state-of-the-art academic and dance training facilities.

November 24, 2002

Power to the People

The provincial government's recent plan to open the electricity market to the private sector must have had poor old Adam Beck spinning in his Hamilton, Ontario, grave since it was Beck who devoted most of his life trying to wrestle this lucrative commodity away from its original promoters, a collection of very powerful and very rich private entrepreneurs.

To be fair, without that entrepreneurial spirit the use of electricity, described at the turn of the last century as "the wonder of the age," would not have come to Ontario as early as it did. In fact, in the overall scheme of things Sir Adam Beck and the birth of his Hydro Electric Power Commission of Ontario in 1906 were relative latecomers. Electricity had actually made an appearance in Toronto in the early 1880s thanks to the inventiveness of John Joseph Wright, who had immigrated to Canada from England a few years earlier. Unable to find the type of work he desired, Wright moved to Philadelphia where he obtained employment as a mechanic in a biscuit factory. It was while attending night classes at Philadelphia High School that Wright learned the fundamentals of electricity from two pioneers in the field, Elihu Thomson and Edwin Houston, a partnership that went on to become part of today's mammoth General Electric Company. Wright went on to distinguish himself by helping install the first electric street lighting on the continent in that American city. However, Wright saw

A miniature version of the falls at Niagara was erected over the entrance to City Hall. On the evening of May 11, 1911, the peoples' power company, later known as Ontario Hydro, would supply electricity generated at the falls to power a small pump, causing water to flow over the model falls. Cheap electricity had indeed arrived in Toronto.

his future not in the States, but back in Toronto where electricity was still a virtual unknown. He moved into an undistinguished looking gun and lock shop half-hidden up a laneway at the northeast corner of Yonge and King streets (where the Royal Bank Building now stands). Here, he built an electricity-producing dynamo like the one he had experimented with in the States. The dynamo was powered by the small steam engine that was used by day to turn the lathes in the gun shop. Before long Wright's dynamo was producing sufficient electricity to illuminate a string of fifteen electric arc lights he placed on the telegraph poles that lined nearby King Street. Hundreds gathered to witness the miracle, and before long additional arc lamps were lighting the way up Yonge Street from the waterfront to the modern Dundas Street.

While Wright continued with his various experiments, others were dreaming about the fortunes to be made by exploiting the use of electricity. Locally, a trio of entrepreneurs consisting of Messrs. Mackenzie, Nicolls, and Pellatt (the latter would build Casa Loma some years later) didn't just dream about getting rich. They decided to pool their financial resources, build coal-fired power plants, and sell the electricity to eager customers at a nice profit. However, the real money would come from generating huge amounts of electricity using the free supply of water cascading over the falls at Niagara. This cheap power would then be sold at inflated rates to their customers. Through their Electrical Power Development Company, the trio would soon share riches beyond their wildest dreams. Actually, generating that cheap power was the easy part of the equation. Getting it from Niagara Falls to where it could make the most money, that was more difficult.

By 1896, private interests were able to transmit electricity from the falls to nearby Buffalo. However, the distance was minimal. For the Canadians, Toronto was more than ninety miles from the falls. Nevertheless, the syndicate persevered in its quest, and on November 19, 1906, hydroelectric power generated at Niagara Falls arrived in the provincial capital city. Toronto streetcars, which just happened to be owned by Mr. Mackenzie, used the power, as did many businesses and industries that relied on electrical apparatus made by Fred Nicholls's manufacturing company. The money began to pile up. And there was no competition, at least not yet. In the same year that hydro arrived in Toronto, businessman-turned-politician Adam Beck appeared on the scene. It was his heartfelt belief that access to cheap electricity was the right of every person living in the province, and his newly created Hydro Electric Power Commission of Ontario would see that they got it. As far as Beck was concerned, it was "power to the people" and the private companies be damned. For the next few years Torontonians continued to buy their electricity, at greatly inflated prices, from the private syndicate. But all that changed on May 11, 1911, when, in front of a crowd of more than one hundred thousand happy citizens, Ontario Premier James Whitney and Adam Beck, the people's power champion, jointly turned a switch sending an electric current generated at Niagara Falls through the thousands of small lights strung in front of City Hall and above the Queen and Bay intersection. Night was turned into day. The public had won. Cheap electricity had arrived in Toronto and soon the syndicate would be out of business. Fast forward ninety-one years ... do we never learn from history?

December 1, 2002

Memories of Eaton's

It was exactly 133 years ago this very day, December 8, 1869, that a young man opened the first dry goods store under his own name, T. Eaton & Co. Since his arrival in the province of Canada West (Ontario) from his native Ireland, a nation still staggering under the impact of the potato famine, Timothy Eaton had worked with several family members who had also immigrated to this land of promise in dry goods stores that they had opened in small rural communities like Glen Williams, Kirkton, and St. Mary's.

Early in 1869, a restless Timothy decided it was time he went into business for himself. And if he was going to make that leap, he might as well head to where the action was, the big city of Toronto, population forty-seven thousand. There, Timothy rented space in a small two-storey structure at the southwest corner of Yonge and Queen streets, a somewhat daring choice since it was well away from the then business heart of the young city, along King Street east of Yonge. His Yonge and Queen location would later be occupied by his business rival, Robert Simpson, and is now the site of the main downtown store of Simpson's successor, the Hudson's Bay Company.

Timothy was in command of the T. Eaton business for nearly four decades, his tenure ending suddenly with his death on January 31, 1907, from complications brought on by pneumonia. He rests for all time in the imposing Eaton family mausoleum in Mount Pleasant Cemetery. The

THE TWO STORES
OF THE JUBILEE—
*Eaton's in 1869 and
in 1919*

Courtesy Eaton's Golden Jubilee book; drawing by C.W. Jefferys

Above: Timothy Eaton's first Toronto store, south-west corner of Yonge and Queen streets.

Left: Are those tears in Timothy's eyes? This statue was presented to Timothy's widow by the company staff in 1919, Eaton's Golden Jubilee year. The work was moved to the Royal Ontario Museum in 1999.

company continued to flourish under the leadership of Timothy's son John Craig Eaton, who thought up the idea of the annual Santa Claus parade (the first was held in 1905) and in 1915 was knighted for his patriotic efforts during the Great War. Following Sir John's death in 1922, cousin Edward Young Eaton took up the challenge until Timothy's grandson John David was ready to take over. J.D. resigned in 1969 and died in 1973. With his resignation, the presidency of Eaton's was out of the family's hands until Fredrik, John David's second eldest son, was anointed in 1977. Eleven years later George, Fred's youngest brother, became the last member of the family to be company president. Just when the company's long slide into oblivion actually began has been the speculation of many articles and books (the best account being that found in Rod McQueen's fascinating *The Eatons*, Stoddart, 1998). But the death of Eaton's wasn't quick. The company sort of stumbled along as buyers that might keep the name alive were scouted. In the meantime, to help stop the financial bleeding, several stores were closed. Then in 1999 Sears bought into the company, more stores were eliminated, and those that remained, such as the one in the Eaton Centre (a name that hopefully will always be around to remind us of this remarkable Canadian family), were identified as "eatons." While much has been written about the rise and fall of the Eaton empire (its absolute demise could be said to have occurred on April 18, 2000, when the last items in the Eaton's seventh-floor boardroom were put under the auctioneer's hammer) not much attention has been paid to the thousands who proudly referred to themselves throughout it all as "Eatonians." These were the people behind the counters, on the phones, behind the wheel of the company delivery trucks, and in the warehouses and offices, all of whom made up the real heart and soul of Eaton's. Author Patricia Phenix has changed that oversight in her new book, *The Eatonians: the Story of the Family behind the Family* (McClelland & Stewart, $37.99). Travelling coast to coast, Patricia sought out the stories behind those things that made Eaton's special to the thousands of Eatonians: Shadow Lake Camp, the Eaton's catalogue, the Round Room restaurant, Eaton Auditorium, the Annex, the horse-drawn delivery wagons (after 1936 motorized delivery trucks), and many, many more memories of a time, and a company, that was.

December 8, 2002

Stories from History on Track

At a recent news conference on the future of HMCS *Haida* (incidentally, by the time this column appears *Haida* will probably be at the Port Weller dry dock, where she will undergo extensive refitting before being berthed in Hamilton I met Chris Anderson, a faithful *Sunday Sun* reader and "friend of the *Haida*" who said he would e-mail me several interesting old photographs from his collection and, if I found them of interest, he'd be glad to relate the stories behind the photos, stories that he thought I might like to share with my *Sunday Sun* readers.

As anyone who has e-mail can verify, a slowly materializing image on a computer screen resulting from the transmission over a telephone line of zillions of electronic 0s and 1s has got to be one of the most amazing technological inventions in history. While the downloading took some time (only dial-up service is available in our neighbourhood), it wasn't long before I could see that one of the photos was of a "radial" streetcar (so called because the routes on which this type of vehicle operated radiated out from the city into the suburban countryside) with 2 men posing beside the car. The second view was of a man in what I assumed was some sort of military uniform.

Once I had the photos printed I was eager to contact Chris and learn the rest of the story. Examining the first view it became apparent that the radial car is operating on the old Toronto Suburban Railway's Weston route. The TSR had been established in 1894 as a

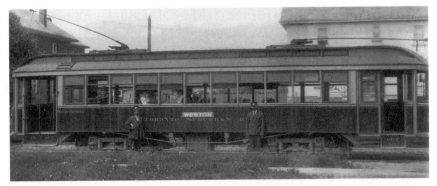

The Toronto Suburban Railway's #18, somewhere on Weston Road, with Conductor Henry James Carter at left, *circa* 1915.

Driver Henry James Carter (1866–1916), at fifty years of age one of the oldest of the sixty thousand Canadians killed in the First World War.

result of the amalgamation of a pair of streetcar companies that had started serving such fast-growing communities such as Carleton, Bracondale, and West Toronto Junction, located out in the city's western suburbs. A year later the company extend its tracks north on Weston Road from the Keele and Dundas intersection to the bustling town of Weston. In 1911, the TSR was acquired by William Mackenzie, who also owned the Toronto Railway Company that provided less-than-perfect public transit service within the big city. The Weston line was eventually extended north almost eight miles from Church Street in Weston to Pine Street in Woodbridge, with big electric radial car #25 (similar to the radial car in the photo) rolling into town in time for the opening of the community's 1914 Fall Fair, a fun-filled event that still takes place each autumn. The Woodbridge extension ceased operating in the spring of 1926, with service on the southern part of the route continued using TTC streetcars (until 1948) and then by trolley coach and now diesel buses.

331

Here's the interesting part of the story. The gentleman to the left in the photo was Chris Anderson's great-grandfather Henry James Carter. A closer look reveals that Henry is holding a "coffee pot" under his arm, thereby identifying him as the conductor of this two-man car. The identity of the other fellow is unknown. Henry was born in England in 1866 and after immigrating to Canada with his parents eventually found employment with the Toronto Suburban Railway. Soon after the outbreak of the Great War, Henry attempted to join the Canadian Army. But at forty-eight years of age, he was well over the maximum age limit of forty-five. Undaunted, Henry fudged his vital statistics and came up with a revised birth date in the year 1871. That made him, in the army's eyes anyway, forty-four years of age. He was quickly signed up and assigned as a driver in the Royal Canadian Horse Artillery. Henry James Carter fell at the Battle of the Somme; he had just turned fifty, one of the oldest Canadians to fall in the carnage that was to enter the history books as the First World War.

December 15, 2002

Streetcar-Only Lanes

Just when I think I'm going to have difficulty coming up with another idea for this column (I've written almost thirteen hundred of them since joining the *Sunday Sun* a quarter of a century ago), I can count on some city official to come up with a "revolutionary" new civic improvement scheme. What makes the supposedly new scheme fodder for this column is the fact that in many cases the idea has been tried before.

A case in point is a plan that would see streetcar-only lanes installed on St. Clair Avenue between Yonge and Keele streets. Special concrete curbing, like that found on the streetcar right- of-way on Spadina Avenue, would keep cars and trucks out of the way, thereby enabling the transit vehicle (some like to call it them "light rail vehicles," but to most Torontonians the familiar term "streetcar" will do) to do its job, moving lots of people as fast and efficiently as possible. Turn lanes and advance greens would help speed the motorized stuff on its way. As is often the case, ideas that seem brand new are often merely a revival of plans and schemes tried by our predecessors. Some stick, others are abandoned and forgotten. In fact, the concept of reserved streetcar lanes on St. Clair Avenue is not a new idea. It was almost a century ago that the city officials of the day decided to initiate a new streetcar route along what was nothing more than a dusty east-west concession road (known to many as simply The Third) located well north of the busy city. The determination to build this line, which would be part of the new city-sponsored Civic Railway system,

The streetcar-only boulevard is clearly visible in this *circa* 1923 view of St. Clair Avenue between Avenue Road (that's Deer Park United Church just east of the Avenue Road intersection at top centre) and Warren Road. The photo was taken from the roof of Timothy Eaton Memorial Church.

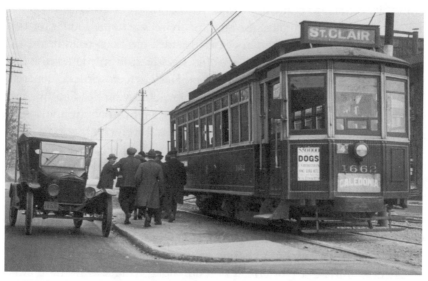

Ex-TRC wooden car #1662 was in use from 1910 to 1951 and is seen here at St. Clair and Bathurst Street *circa* 1924, a period of time when the centre reservation was in use.

was a result of the then privately owned transit operator's refusal to extend its routes into the less populated (and therefore less financially appealing) suburbs, in this instance places like Deer Park, Bracondale, Earlscourt, and Silverthorn. While the populations of these small communities were growing, it was the view of the owners of the Toronto Railway Company that even taken together they weren't large enough to justify the expense of building a new streetcar line to serve them. And so the city did, opening its new St. Clair line on August 13, 1913. The terminals were Yonge Street on the east and Station Street (a small street a little west of Lansdowne at the Grand Trunk railway crossing) on the west.

Before construction actually began on the new line, and in anticipation of the future growth of the city, civic officials agreed that now was the time to widen St. Clair Avenue while at the same time placing the new streetcar tracks within a thirty-three-foot-wide boulevard where they'd be protected from an ever-increasing number of "gas buggies" by concrete curbing. The Yonge to Avenue Road stretch was widened to from its original sixty-six-foot width to eighty-six feet (houses that had already been built along this part of St. Clair made acquiring any more land prohibitive), while the less populated section from Avenue Road westerly to the Grand Trunk tracks was widened an additional fourteen feet, making it one hundred feet wide. This foresight accounts for the street's expansive look today.

In 1928, the increased traffic in the business section between Bathurst and Dufferin resulted in the centre boulevard being removed with the Dufferin to Lansdowne boulevard vanishing the next year. Then came the Great Depression. In an attempt to get men back to work, a number of unemployment relief projects were discussed by the various levels of government. One such project that was approved, at a cost of $419,392, was the removal of the remaining length of boulevard on St. Clair Avenue West, the sixty-six-hundred-foot stretch between Yonge and Bathurst. By the end of 1935, the "streetcar only" reservation on St. Clair was gone.

Some years ago there was talk about eliminating all streetcar operations in Toronto with the last route, St. Clair, becoming history by 1980. My, how things change! The St. Clair streetcar is not only still there (and busier than ever), they're now talking about resurrecting the streetcar-only centre boulevard at a cost of $7 million. And they may even extend the St. Clair route to Jane Street!

December 22, 2002

On the Waterfront

If you've become as confused as I have over just what our city's waterfront will look like ten, twenty, even thirty years from now, join the growing masses. In fact, the subject of what to do with Toronto's waterfront has been a subject of discussion for almost as long as Toronto has been a city. One of the first attempts to bring some control over what up until then had been years and years of haphazard planning occurred in 1911 with the birth of the new Toronto Harbour Commission. Its mandate was to bring order out of chaos through the orderly development of the waterfront between Victoria Park Avenue on the east and the Humber River on the west. Three separate land uses were given equal treatment in this comprehensive multi-million-dollar redevelopment scheme: industrial in the eastern harbour area (Ashbridge's Bay), commercial in the central waterfront area (either side of the foot of Yonge Street), and recreational in the area west of Bathurst Street and out along the beaches adjacent to the old Humber Bay.

As part of this latter development, a new traffic artery, to be known as the Boulevard Drive, would be constructed atop land reclaimed from the lake. This modern thoroughfare would eventually connect with Fleet Street (another new traffic artery that was built to serve the central part of the waterfront development) at Bathurst Street. Together they provided a "high-speed" cross-waterfront route over the Humber River joining Parliament Street on the east with the recently con-

Work progresses on the new Tip Top Tailors building on the Boulevard Drive, 1929. The landmark structure is being converted into the tiptoplofts, where condominium prices will range from $164,000 to $1.3 million.

structed Toronto-Hamilton Highway on the west. Some suggested that one day the Boulevard Drive would be diverted under the Western Gap in a tunnel, run the length of Toronto Island, and return to the mainland via a bridge (!!) over the Eastern Gap, where it would connect with what is now Cherry Street. Obviously this has never happened (at least not yet), and in 1960 the Fleet Street/Boulevard Drive combo was officially renamed Lake Shore Boulevard, the name by which we know it today. It wasn't long after the new Boulevard Drive was announced that plans were being prepared for buildings that would take advantage of this new traffic artery.

Loblaw's Groceterias' new plant and warehouse at the northeast corner of Bathurst and the Boulevard Drive opened in 1928 while across just across the drive the Crosse and Blackwell jams and pickles people had moved into their place a year earlier. The two joined the new Maple Leaf Stadium in which the city's professional Triple A baseball team began playing its home games in the spring of 1926. The first two structures are still there, while the stadium vanished in a cloud of dust in 1968. The fourth member of the quartet of new buildings to take advantage of the new Boulevard Drive was the million-dollar Tip Top Tailors building, in which were found manufacturing facilities, company offices, and showrooms.

The company's building formed the backdrop for this *circa* 1935 newspaper ad.

Tip Top Tailors had been established by Benjamin Dunkleman in 1910. The company's catchy name came as a result of a contest, with a Mr. Peabody winning twenty-five dollars for his submission. Eventually the company outgrew its Adelaide Street West Factory, and in 1929 it moved into its magnificent new building on the Boulevard Drive. It was in this building that virtually all the uniforms for Canada's Second World War personnel (as well as those of some Russian soldiers) were made. Years later Tip Top became part of the Dylex Diversified organization, and it is now part of Grafton Fraser Inc.

December 29, 2002

Views of Toronto's Evolving Skyline